STAMP STENCIL PAINT

MAKING EXTRAORDINARY
PATTERNED PROJECTS BY HAND

ANNA JOYCE

PHOTOGRAPHY BY LISA WARNINGER
PHOTOSTYLING BY CHELSEA FUSS

STC CRAFT / A MELANIE FALICK BOOK / NEW YORK

Published in 2015 by Stewart, Tabori & Chang
An imprint of ABRAMS

Library of Congress Control Number: 2014959128
ISBN: 978-1-61769-177-5

Editors: Melanie Falick and Valerie Shrader
Designer: Brooke Reynolds for inchmark
Production Manager: Anet Sirna-Bruder

The text of this book was composed in Avenir.

Printed and bound in China.

10 9 8 7 6 5 4 3 2 1

Stewart, Tabori & Chang books are available at special discounts when purchased in quantity for premiums and promotions as well as fundraising or educational use. Special editions can also be created to specification. For details, contact specialsales@abramsbooks.com or the address below.

ABRAMS
THE ART OF BOOKS SINCE 1949

115 West 18th Street
New York, NY 10011
www.abramsbooks.com

For my parents.

CONTENTS

INTRODUCTION

I AM THE ONLY CHILD OF TWO ARTISTS. WHEN I WAS A BABY MY MOTHER WOULD TAKE ME TO HER TINY PRINTMAKING STUDIO ON THE THIRD FLOOR OF AN OLD BUILDING IN DOWNTOWN EUGENE, OREGON, IN A BACKPACK.

Some of my earliest memories are from there—her cutting tools, her stacks of fluffy white rag paper waiting for colorful prints, the smell of ink rolled out onto sheets of glass. When I was a little older I would go to my father's photography studio. As we watched the black-and-white photographs magically appear, he would play records from his prized collection and talk to me about life and music—jazz, blues, classic rock 'n' roll.

Growing up I always had art supplies on hand. As a teenager I spent much of my time in a studio my parents made for me in a spare bedroom in our home, working on collages, paintings, and elaborate handmade cards and gifts. In college, at the California College of the Arts in Oakland, California, I studied printmaking. I was inspired by patterns and colors from vintage books and the fabrics, ribbons, paper, and ceramics I would gather in thrift shops. Although I did most of my work on paper, I took a class in the textile department on a whim, and fell hopelessly in love with fabric and weaving, too.

After graduating I didn't have access to a printmaking studio but wanted to continue my art practice. Fortunately, as a wedding gift, my husband, Victor, and I had been given a sewing machine and a small wicker basket filled with needles, thread, and a good pair of scissors. My mother taught me how to thread the machine, my father built me a sewing table (which I still use today), and after the first few stitches, everything that inspired me suddenly came together: print, pattern, color, and textiles. I spent the next ten years teaching myself how to sew. Then, in 2009, encouraged by my husband and mother, I started my own business selling hand-printed textiles. My first collection was comprised of simple cloth napkins, table runners, and pillows.

When I was given the incredible opportunity to write *Stamp Stencil Paint*, I knew I wanted to design projects for many surfaces: fabric, ceramics, leather, metal, and even walls. There was no surface that did not inspire me! As soon as I started working on the book, I couldn't stop imagining patterns applied everywhere. When I told the people at Collage, my favorite local art supply shop, about *Stamp Stencil Paint*, they generously offered to sponsor supplies. And then West Elm was kind enough to donate products for me to use for some of the projects. It was time to get started on a collection of patterns.

Although I had been shopping in art supply shops for years, somehow I hadn't noticed some of the new tools available. Now it was my JOB to try them out. I found new hand-stamping materials, stamp pads in amazing colors that were designed to be used on many surfaces, light-sensitive dyes that could be applied to fabric, new stenciling tools, and paints of all kinds in beautiful premixed colors. Each day, back in my home studio, I felt my creative energy rising. In addition to trying out my new supplies, I started exploring new techniques and refreshing my memory about the ones I had learned during childhood and in college. I loved how quickly I could go from feeling inspired to seeing results because printing and painting patterns by hand is so simple. Overall, my goal was to choose and present easy techniques and projects that would inspire everyone to add more pattern to their lives by making what they want and need with their own hands. Each chapter of *Stamp Stencil Paint* begins with a basic overview of the technique featured and a description of tools and supplies, then moves on to the projects and instructions. Although you could approach the projects in this book sequentially, I imagine that you're more likely to

choose projects based on what you like and the kind of mood you're in. While stamping is a pretty forgiving medium and doesn't usually require too much precision, stenciling requires a certain straightforward discipline. So, if you're feeling like making a quick afternoon project, you might want to stamp some colorful throw pillows (see page 38) or decorate a set of terra cotta pots for your patio or garden (see page 51). If you have a little more time, I suggest diving into the stencil chapter and printing a pattern with multiple colors, such as the stylish tote bag (page 66) or the bright table linens (page 70). Painting requires the least number of tools, but the most spirit to execute. While you need to watch where the paint goes, the looser and freer you are feeling when you apply it, the more natural and satisfying your results are likely to be. Whatever project you choose, relax and enjoy the process and remember that the inconsistencies and "imperfections" that come from your hands are a significant part of what make all of these techniques so special.

Of course, I hope that you will want to make every project in the book, but on days when you can't actually make time for crafting, I hope that just flipping the pages will please you and spark your creative spirit.

This book is meant to be joyous. It is about trying something new, embracing "imperfections," and most of all, taking the time to create by hand.

I made this for you.

Top left, the patina on my studio work table; top right, hiding in my mother's printmaking studio; above, a photo of my mother and me in her studio, taken by my father.

GETTING STARTED

EACH PROJECT IN *STAMP STENCIL PAINT* WAS DESIGNED TO BE SIMPLE, EFFECTIVE, AND DELIVER GREAT RESULTS. FOR SOME PROJECTS YOU WILL NEED TO KNOW BASIC SEWING SKILLS, OR PURCHASE A FEW SPECIAL SUPPLIES, BUT MOST REQUIRE JUST THE COURAGE TO JUMP IN AND GET STARTED. YOU WILL NEED TO RELIEVE YOURSELF OF FEAR AND SIMPLY MAKE A PATTERN, BY HAND, AND I WILL SHOW YOU HOW. HERE IS A BRIEF OVERVIEW OF WHAT YOU CAN EXPECT FROM EACH CHAPTER.

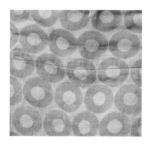

STAMP As a printmaker, I have a soft spot in my heart for stamps. I use my own hand-carved stamps, and I love watching the pattern grow with each impression. Stamping is very immediate—you can carve a simple one in a few minutes and then use it for years, building a library of patterns as you go. Hand stamping is also a meditation on embracing the unexpected. No matter how consistent you are, each impression is unique and that uniqueness breathes life into your patterns. These projects are fun, lighthearted, and playful. In this chapter I show you how to create patterns on ceramics, leather, paper, and more!

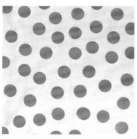

STENCIL A stencil is an incredible way to create clean, crisp, intricate patterns and apply them to a vast array of surfaces. Stencils are ideal for designs that use multiple colors, so your patterns can become increasingly complex. In this chapter I show you how to hand-cut stencils from patterns I have designed and also how to use commercial stencils, such as architectural drafting templates. You will learn how to build beautiful floral and geometric prints for surfaces ranging from textiles and ceramics to furniture and walls.

PAINT The projects in this chapter are less about learning a specific technique and more about gaining the confidence to dive in, play with color, and build a pattern from scratch. Most people feel a certain amount of anxiety at the thought of taking a brush to an object and simply painting on it. But if you conquer that fear, you will discover how lovely, stylish, and full of life an imperfect, wiggly, possibly even crooked handmade pattern can be! The painting projects I present will teach you how to embellish surfaces such as ceramics, paper, and cloth—you can even paint bold, stylish bedding for your home. The tools for this chapter include paint and brushes—as well as the confidence to use them.

CREATING A COLOR STORY

I have never been one to shy away from unusual or vibrant color combinations in my work, so my personal color theory has always been "If you love it, it matches." But there are a few tips and tricks for choosing colors that I return to again and again when developing patterns, regardless of whether I'm stamping, stenciling, or painting.

When I am working on a design for a new pattern I will often have a color, or a collection of colors, in mind before I get started. These are called "color stories." If you are working on a project for a new baby you may want your color story to be bright and cheerful, and pick fun, vibrant colors like orange and green as I did for the Simple Cotton Quilt on page 122. If you have something more understated in mind, timeless colors like cobalt blue, rich chocolate brown, or black would be a good place to start.

When adding pattern to an object that will be installed permanently or live in a room with many other colors and patterns, such as the Folk Art Barn Lamp on page 74, consider picking a more neutral and low-key color such as a classic navy blue. It will help the pattern stand the test of time and not compete for attention with the rest of the space. If the project is something that will be enjoyed and then put away until the next use, such as the Coral Dots Dessert Plates on page 108, do not be afraid to use a bold and dramatic color and let it be the star of the show.

Another consideration when choosing hues is the color and texture of the ground (or surface) you are working on. For instance, I wanted the quality and beauty of the linen to really shine in the Circles Linen Apron (page 26), so I chose a semitransparent ink in a cheerful blue that would complement, and not compete with, the tones of the raw linen. Another example of this is the Patterned Terra Cotta Pots (page 51). The dark, absorbent clay made the shades slightly duller, so I used very bright and saturated colors to give my patterns more pop.

When working with two colors in a design, you can almost never go wrong picking one vibrant shade (such as sunshine yellow or bright pink) and pairing it with a darker, more neutral color. In the Windswept Bedding Set (page 130), a bright yellow gets a dose of sophistication when paired with a dark charcoal gray. For the Floral Tote Bag (page 66 and pictured above right), a salmon pink is tempered with a dusky navy

Don't be afraid to use color in your designs. Experiment with combinations to develop a color story for each project, such as the blue and pink motif used on the Floral Tote Bag (page 66).

blue, giving the bag a huge dose of color without making it difficult to pair with the other hues in your wardrobe.

Another go-to combination for me is using colors in the same family. For the Painterly Party Clutch (page 118) I chose a bright pink paint and even brighter pink leather. I used this technique again for the Brushstroke Kitchen Linens (page 104), using tones in the blue-green family to create a "matching" set.

You can best educate yourself about color by experimenting. Pick colors that you are drawn to, test them, and have fun! And when in doubt, a warm charcoal gray looks good with just about anything.

WHY SCALE MATTERS

Scale refers to the size of the pattern, and is usually broken down into three simple categories—small, medium, and large. Often, very small objects call for small-scale patterns, as you see in the Anemone Salt Cellar on page 115, and larger projects need larger-scale patterns. Very large areas covered in small-scale patterns can look too busy and overwhelm the eye.

When I am designing a pattern, I strive for balance. I want the eye to move all over the finished design without any one spot looking too dense or too sparse. One helpful exercise that my mother taught me years ago is to take a step back from your work and squint your eyes. Are there areas that immediately jump out to you as looking too empty or too full? Are there spots that feel visually heavy or tight? This trick can help you balance your design for a more successful project.

Like most "rules" in design, however, there are exceptions. The patterns in *Stamp Stencil Paint* are meant to be used and enjoyed. Experiment with them! Try a large motif on a small object for fresh and playful results. Or print a small-scale pattern scattered over a large surface to see how it looks and feels. The more patterns you work with, the better you will become at scaling them.

SUPPLIES

Here I present an overview of basic materials and tools you will need for patternmaking. See the individual chapters for the more specific information you will need before starting a project.

PIGMENT

The term "pigment" is often used in a generic way to describe the substance that provides color. It could be paint, ink, markers—what have you. When I use the word "pigment" in this book, I use it in that basic sense of adding color. Each particular pigment should be carefully chosen according to its unique properties.

All-surface acrylic paints or textile paints are all you need in the majority of projects in *Stamp Stencil Paint*, but other pigment is occasionally used: for example, an ink pad is used in the stamping chapter to create the pattern on the Circles Linen Apron (page 26). You will learn more about other types of pigment as needed throughout the individual chapters.

All-Surface Acrylic Paint

For many of the projects, I used acrylic paints, which can be applied to multiple surfaces. Although there are paints designed for specific surfaces, I like using the more versatile all-surface acrylic paints when possible. They are inexpensive and come in a huge variety of colors, which is great if you prefer using a color right out of the jar rather than mixing your own shades. My favorite brand is the Martha Stewart Multi-Surface Satin Acrylic Craft Paint.

All-surface acrylic paints are saturated and opaque, which creates bright, bold color. They tend to stiffen when dry, so they work best on leather, ceramic, or very thick fabrics where the texture of the paint will not compete with the texture of the finished project.

Textile Paint

Not surprisingly, textile paint is usually the best choice when stamping or stenciling on fabric because it does not stiffen as acrylic paint does. It rolls out easily with a brayer and stamps well, but does not usually change the texture of the fabric.

Like acrylic paints, textile paints come in a wide variety of colors and can be custom-mixed to produce an infinite number of shades. To maintain colorfastness, textile paints must be heat-set according to the manufacturer's directions. The small jars containing 2.25 ounces (66.5 ml) are generally sufficient for the projects in this book; if more than one jar is required, the instructions provide this information.

For hand painting or dyeing fabric, I use a textile paint called Dye-Na-Flow. It is technically a paint but behaves like a dye because it flows freely and yields beautiful saturated color. It is meant to be applied with a brush or used for soaking textiles in a bath of color.

> **COLORS THAT FLATTER:** Shades of blue and pink complement nearly all skin tones and are almost universally flattering. That's why I like to use them when I'm creating projects that will be worn close to the face, such as the Solar Print Scarf (page 126) and Silk Infinity Scarf (page 82).

MIXING CUSTOM COLORS

I often choose to use an all-surface acrylic or textile paint in a premixed color. However, depending on the project you choose, it may be necessary to mix paint colors together to reach the shade I used or the one you desire. Color recipes are included in the project instructions when needed, but here is a primer on how to mix custom colors.

· Use a clean plastic cup, artist palette, or a plastic paint tray with multiple wells for mixing your paint. I prefer to use a paintbrush for mixing colors. The flexible bristles blend paint efficiently and you can quickly test your colors as you mix them, as you already have the appropriate tool in your hand.

· As a general rule, start with the lightest color of paint and slowly add the darker color until you reach your desired shade.

· Make sure to stir well after mixing colors so your finished project does not end up with streaks.

· Mix enough color to finish your project, because it is often difficult to replicate a custom color. Note that acrylic paint will usually dry one to two shades darker on fabric and liquid textile paints will dry several shades lighter, so always allow the paint to dry completely before you decide on a final mix.

ACRYLIC ARTIST PALETTE

For mixing and rolling pigment and printing and painting patterns, I recommend an 8½ x 11-inch (21.6 x 27.9 cm) sheet of acrylic (also called Plexiglas). These inexpensive sheets are available at art stores. You can see me using one on page 23.

BRUSHES AND APPLICATORS

A variety of brushes and other applicators for pigment can be used for patternmaking, from small fine-tipped paintbrushes for touch-ups to wide bristle brushes for creating large swaths of color. I even used a brayer—a rolling tool for applying pigment—as a "brush" in the Brayer Print Wall Art project on page 112. Invest in quality brushes that do not shed bristles easily; these will last a very long time and provide better results than cheap brushes. Specific brush requirements are provided in each set of project instructions.

UTILITY KNIFE

A utility knife is an invaluable tool for making stamps and stencils. It will allow you to "draw" around the templates in a fluid motion and can create smaller, more detailed shapes than scissors can. Get a utility knife that is about the size of a pen, not the larger box cutter. You need to change blades often to get the cleanest lines for your designs, so keep a good supply on hand. Even though it may seem counterintuitive, a sharp blade is much easier and safer to use than a dull one. When using a utility knife, make sure to always keep a keen eye on the task at hand so you do not cut yourself.

SHARP SCISSORS

A pair of sharp scissors is needed for general cutting tasks as well as for making stencils.

CUTTING MAT

A large, self-healing cutting mat is an indispensable tool when working with fabric, since it has a grid that makes measuring and cutting a breeze. But it is also helpful when making your own stencils and carving stamps. A cutting mat protects your work area from nicks and cuts, and provides a cushioned surface that makes using a utility knife easier and safer. I prefer to use a 24 x 36-inch (61 x 91.4 cm) mat so I can cut in large strokes without having to worry that my blade will slip off the edge onto an unprotected surface.

Store your cutting mat flat and out of direct sunlight, and never use it as an ironing surface. Excessive heat will make your cutting mat buckle and render it useless.

MEASURING TOOLS

A plain wooden ruler will work just fine for most of the projects in this book, but one of my favorite tools is a transparent acrylic quilting ruler. I like being able to see through the ruler onto my project, especially if I am using the edge to draw lines or create patterns using a pen or brush. Acrylic rulers come in all lengths and widths, but the one I use most is about 4 x 14 inches (10.2 x 35.6 cm).

ARTIST TAPE

Artist tape is a particular type of tape that is repositionable and does not leave any sticky residue on your surface. It works well on all surfaces including paper, as it can be removed easily without damage. Artist tape is also great to use as a resist for painting and stenciling, as you can see in the Striped Storage Basket (page 90). Artist tape comes in many colors and several widths—one roll of ½-inch (1.3 cm) tape will serve you well in every chapter of this book.

STUDIO APRON

Painting, printing, and stamping can be messy, so a good studio apron is a must to protect your clothing. There is also great satisfaction to be had from watching fingerprints and colors build up a patina on your apron as you move further into a project.

CANVAS DROP CLOTH

Canvas drop cloths are inexpensive and easy to find at any hardware or art supply store. They will protect your work surface or floor and make cleanup much easier.

SKETCHBOOK AND DESIGN FOLDER

A sketchbook for taking notes, doodling, drawing, and saving swatches of color will be very useful as you move through this book. It will be an invaluable resource of inspiration to help you develop new ideas. I also recommend you keep a folder of all the stencils and templates you use because they can be repurposed and will be at the ready when you are suddenly inspired to make something.

A PLACE TO MAKE

I feel very strongly about the importance of having a place where you can make things. I have always called that place a "studio," but I define that term loosely. A studio can be a place where you make for an afternoon, a weekend, or a lifetime. Because my children are young, I keep my studio at home. My family lives in a small cozy house in the heart of the city, and when I began creating the projects for this book, it became apparent that I needed a second studio separate from the place where I sew and run my textile design business. After a weekend of working upstairs in our dining room, my husband suggested that I take over the room and use it as my "book studio."

I designed and finished every project that you see in this book at the family table. A little to my surprise, my daughters delighted in this new studio and had an innate respect for my tools and projects that were in various stages of completion. They stamped on scraps of paper while I was working, and then wandered off (usually with some brightly colored tape) to create something of their own nearby. So when I say that you can make every project in this book at your dining room or kitchen table, I really do mean it!

I suggest finding a place that inspires you, where you feel comfortable and have a bit of room to move around. Being near a window is lovely, and a sturdy work surface such as a table or desk is a must. Before you begin a project, take a moment to rid your new "studio" of clutter, read though all of the project instructions, and arrange all of your supplies so they are close at hand. There is nothing worse than getting started only to find out that your supplies are not in order.

STAMP

STAMPING BASICS

A HAND-STAMPED PRINT IS FORMED BY APPLYING PRESSURE TO A BLOCK OF MATERIAL THAT HAS AN IMAGE CARVED INTO IT. THE TRADITIONAL MATERIALS FOR MAKING PRINTS ARE LINOLEUM OR WOOD, BUT NOW THERE ARE MODERN SUBSTANCES FOR MAKING STAMPS THAT ARE MUCH EASIER AND FASTER TO CARVE WHILE STILL DELIVERING BEAUTIFUL HAND-PRINTED RESULTS. I LOVE PRINTING WITH STAMPS, AND WHEN YOU SEE HOW EASY IT IS TO BUILD BEAUTIFUL PATTERNS WITH STAMPING, I THINK YOU WILL LOVE IT, TOO.

ANATOMY OF A STAMP

Stamps are made from a material that has been carved, molded, or cut, leaving behind a design or shape that is in relief, or raised. That raised area is then coated with pigment and pressed onto paper, fabric, or some other surface, transferring the image of the carved design. The basic function and design of stamps is very simple, but there is artistry in the process: You must choose the appropriate design and the right stamp material, carve it with care, and pick the correct inks and supplies to have a successful project. There is nuance involved as well; for example, printing on smooth clay is very different than printing on thick textured fabric. I explore all of these ideas in this chapter.

STAMPING SUPPLIES AND TOOLS

Carving your own stamps is much easier than you might imagine. Here are the materials and tools you need to get started.

RUBBER CARVING BLOCKS

High-density rubber blocks are an easy, inexpensive material with which to create handmade stamps. This material is similar to an eraser, and it is quicker, easier, and safer to carve than the rigid surface of linoleum, as it is less likely that your cutting tool will slip. You can cut these soft rubber blocks into solid shapes with a utility knife for graphic geometric prints, or use carving tools (page 20) to create more intricate designs. The stamps you make from these rubber blocks can be used repeatedly and they clean up easily with soap and water. Several companies make rubber blocks for carving; I am fond of two products from Speedball: Speedy-Cut and Speedy-Carve blocks. Pink Speedy-Carve blocks are thin and flexible and can be cut into smaller pieces easily, but they are a little more expensive than white Speedy-Cut blocks, which are less resilient and can crumble a bit over time. Both are very easy to carve and are available in different sizes, so you might consider trying one of each to find out which you prefer.

MOLDABLE FOAM STAMPS

One of my favorite materials for carving stamps is called Magic Stamp. This product is usually used to create stamps by heating the surface and pressing an object into it, but I discovered that it cuts beautifully. I use a utility knife to cut the dense blue 3 x 4-inch (7.6 x 10.2 cm) blocks of foam into simple shapes for stamping. This material is thirsty and soaks in pigment, so it works equally well with all-surface acrylic paint or textile paint and delivers smooth, even, color-rich prints.

STAMPING TOOLS AND MATERIALS:

1. Soft lead pencil 2. Moldable foam stamp 3. Japanese carving tools 4. Acrylic artist palette 5. White artist tape 6. Rubber carving block 7. Utility knife 8. Bone folder 9. Design templates 10. Carving tool with interchangeable blades 11. Hand-carved stamps 12. Brayer 13. All-surface stamp pads 14. All-surface acrylic paints

I like to use foam stamps for printing large allover geometric patterns, and they work especially well for textile and paper projects. The foam is very soft and porous, allowing you to place less pressure on the stamp, which saves your wrists from strain when you are working with a big motif. In some of the project instructions I suggest having multiple blocks, so you can have a separate block for each color and/or design used to make the pattern.

STAMPING KIT

Each set of instructions includes a list of specific supplies, but the items below are needed for virtually every stamping project. Arrange them nearby when you begin working.

· Canvas drop cloth

· Utility knife with extra blades

· Linoleum-carving tools

· Scissors

· Self-healing cutting mat

· Ruler and/or yardstick

· Plastic or paper cups for mixing ink

· Plastic spoons

· Acrylic artist palette

· Bone folder or smooth wooden spoon

· Artist tape

· White paper for tracing designs

· Scrap paper

COMMERCIAL STAMPS

If I am inspired to use an image that is very small and precise, I tend to use purchased rubber stamps because these patterns generally have very fine lines that are difficult to hand-carve. Well-stocked art and craft stores offer an amazing array of pre-made rubber stamps, and you can use them again and again, just as you would a stamp that you made yourself. They are perfect to use when you are pressed for time but want to add a personal touch to a project.

INK PADS

An easy way to apply color to the surface of your stamp is by using purchased stamp pads. There is an almost infinite array of colors and opacities available now since many companies are offering stamp pads with inks that print permanently on surfaces such as fabric, leather, ceramics, and wood as well as paper. Stamp pads are best suited for inking rubber stamps that fit inside the perimeter of the ink pad; a typical case is about 2½ x 4 inches (6.4 x 10.2 cm).

ACRYLIC ARTIST PALETTE

I recommended using an acrylic artist palette in Getting Started (page 14), but I want to emphasize that it is indispensable for mixing colors and rolling out paint into an even layer in preparation for stamping by hand. It cleans up easily in the sink when you are ready to change colors and is very sturdy. Resist the urge to use an old cookie sheet or paper plates and make the small investment in a proper mixing and rolling surface instead. Paper plates will absorb pigment and dry it out while transferring lint onto your brayer and stamp, and the dark surface of a baking sheet makes it difficult to get an accurate idea of your color.

LINOLEUM-CARVING TOOL SET

Although designed for working on traditional linoleum surfaces, linoleum-carving tools are also used for cutting and carving stamps made from rubber. Generally these tools have wooden handles and are sold in a set of individual knives that each have a differently shaped blade—from small V-shaped gouges for detailed line work to larger, almost flat U-shaped blades for clearing away large areas from the stamping surface.

You can also purchase a kit with interchangeable blades that are stored inside a hollow plastic handle when not in use. This is a useful and economical option when you are starting out

(Speedball makes a nice set), but I prefer to work with a set of individual knives because I like being able to pick up the tool I need without having to unscrew the tip and change out the blade. Most of the sets I favor are made in Japan and can be found at specialty printmaking supply stores (see Resources on page 142). These knives are more durable and precise than the interchangeable blades, and they can be sharpened, making them a purchase that will last a lifetime.

BRAYERS

These tools are used to roll paint onto a stamp for printing. The process is simple: You coat the brayer with paint by rolling it on a mixing surface and then transfer the pigment to the stamp. Brayers are available in a range of sizes from 1½ to 8 inches (3.8 to 20.3 cm) and in both acrylic and rubber; acrylic brayers are generally used for burnishing and similar tasks while rubber brayers are well suited for applying pigment and should be used for the projects in *Stamp Stencil Paint*.

I prefer to use a rubber brayer that is about 1½ inches (3.8 cm) wide. This size is wide enough to use on the surface of a large stamp, but not so large that it creates a mess when working with smaller stamps that have fine lines and details.

Brayers are easy to clean and can be used for many years if taken care of properly. After using a brayer, roll it on scrap paper to remove excess pigment and/or wipe away remaining ink as needed. Wash with soap and water and let dry completely before storing.

POSITIVE IMAGE, NEGATIVE SPACE

When you create a rubber stamp, you are carving away negative space, so any areas that you remove will not transfer pigment. You can use this as a design element when you are making your own stamps because you can choose to make your pattern a positive image (cutting away all the background material) or a negative image (cutting away the design itself and leaving the background as your image).

MAKING AND USING STAMPS

Since I use two primary methods for making handmade stamps—carving rubber blocks and cutting moldable foam—instructions for using each technique are provided. The process varies according to the material.

PREPARE THE WORK AREA

A drop cloth is a great way to keep paint off your work area and can be used many, many times. Get ready to work by organizing all your tools beforehand, so your creative time is not interrupted. Be sure to do all your carving and cutting on a self-healing cutting mat.

Before you begin your project, test your stamp and pigment to ensure you're getting the desired effect.

TRANSFER THE DESIGN

Rubber Carving Blocks

If you are carving a stamp from a rubber block, copy the template onto a standard 8½ x 11-inch (21.6 cm x 27.9 cm) piece of paper. Trace over the design with a soft lead pencil. **(A)** Center the tracing lead-side down on the rubber block and rub the back of the paper with a bone folder to transfer the image onto the block. (If you do not have a bone folder, the back of a smooth wooden spoon or your thumbnail will also work well.) **(B)**

 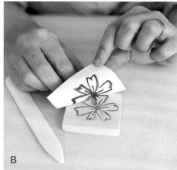

Moldable Foam Stamps

If you are cutting a stamp out of moldable foam, trace the template onto a sheet of white paper and cut out the shape. If the shape is a very simple one, you can just trace around the shape with an utility knife. **(C)**

If the design is more complex, use a little bit of tape to secure the cutout to the top of the foam. Trace around the template with a soft lead pencil—it will make a visible impression in the foam block—and then remove the paper. Wipe away the pencil lead with a damp cloth before printing.

CARVE THE STAMP

Rubber Carving Blocks

When carving a rubber block to create a stamp, use linoleum cutting tools for detailed designs or a utility knife for solid shapes. After you have transferred the design, use the utility knife to cut around the perimeter of the design.

Use the appropriate linoleum-carving tool; remember that the V-shaped blades are best for creating details while the U-shaped blades are often best for carving away curved shapes and removing large areas from a design. Hold the tool in your hand with the end resting in your palm and the blade facing up. Slowly carve away from your body, applying even pressure to the tool. **(D)** Carefully cut away all the material except the transferred design, leaving it in relief. Use the utility knife to cut the excess material from the perimeter of the stamp. **(E)** If you have large scraps remaining, save them to make another stamp.

Moldable Foam Stamps

If you are carving a moldable foam block, use a utility knife to cut the block into the desired shape. This is very simple—just follow the line you traced around the template, using an up-and-down sawing motion. Peel back the foam gently as you work and continue sawing through the block until it separates, creating the stamp. **(F)** It is especially important to use a new, sharp blade when cutting the foam blocks so that they do not tear or leave jagged edges.

Note that whatever image you carve into the surface of your stamp will print in reverse. When you are stamping geometric shapes, the orientation of your design does not matter since there is no "right way" for it to face; none of the design

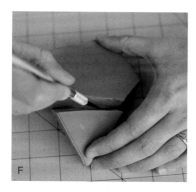

templates in *Stamp Stencil Paint* need to face a particular direction to be effective. But if you would like to carve letters, numbers, or any design that has an obvious "right" way, you need to make sure you transfer the image backwards so it has the correct orientation when printed.

MAKE A TEST PRINT

For more successful stamping projects, it is very important to make test prints on your desired surface. Stamping can be done successfully on a number of different surfaces, as long as they are prepared properly. Fabrics other than canvas should be washed, dried, and ironed (canvas is better to work with if it is not prewashed). If you are working on a ceramic surface, use a clean, damp cloth to remove any dirt or dust from the surface, wipe it with a cotton ball soaked in rubbing alcohol, and let it dry completely before you begin to print. When using a stamp for the first time, you will need to charge it with ink. Charging means applying ink to the surface of the stamp in preparation for printing. This step coats the printing area of your stamp with ink and primes the stamp, giving you more consistent printing results.

When you stamp, applying the right amount of pressure takes a bit of practice. The smaller the stamp, the less pressure you need to apply. For small, commercially made stamps mounted on wood or acrylic, place a medium amount of even pressure to the stamp. For larger, hand-carved solid shapes, press a bit harder using the palm of your hand to get an even print. Applying too much pressure will distort the image and pool the ink, and applying too little will keep your stamp from making full contact with your project surface and result in incomplete prints and faded color.

The techniques for test printing are a little different depending on whether you are using paint from a jar or an ink pad as your pigment.

Test Printing with Paint

Place a small pool of paint about the size of a silver dollar at the top of your mixing surface (preferably a sheet of acrylic, see page 14) and pick up a bit of ink with a brayer. Move to a clean area on the surface and slowly roll your brayer back and forth, picking it up and setting it back down in between revolutions. **(G)** This action will help distribute paint evenly over the surface of the brayer and keep it from simply sliding over the pigment. When you need more paint, pick up some more from the pool and repeat. When the entire surface of the brayer is uniformly covered with paint, roll the brayer across the surface of your stamp several times until it is evenly coated.

Turn the stamp over and lower it slowly onto your test material; ideally this is a little bit of extra fabric or paper from your project. Apply even pressure to the entire surface of the stamp using the palm of your hand. Lift the stamp straight up and set it on your work surface, ink-side up. If the print is too light you may need to add more ink to your stamp or use more pressure when you are printing. **(H)** On the other hand, if there is paint pooling inside or around the perimeter of your stamp you have too much paint or are applying too much pressure. If this happens, rinse and dry your stamp and then continue test printing until you have even, consistent prints.

Test Printing with an Ink Pad

Press the stamp firmly onto the ink pad several times until you see that it is fully coated with ink. **(I)** Turn the stamp over and place it ink-side down onto your test surface; again, it is best to use excess material from your project to get the most accurate results. Press the back of the stamp firmly with your palm and hold it there for several seconds. Lift your stamp straight up and examine your test print. If the print is too light you may need more ink, more pressure on the back of the stamp, or both; if ink is spilling beyond the stamp, try the opposite. Continue inking and stamping until you find the right ratio of ink and pressure. **(J)**

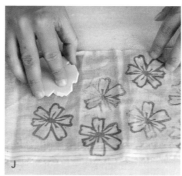

PRINT THE PROJECTS

When you are creating projects in this chapter, you will most often be using the techniques you have just read about. If you need any more specific information that will help you stamp each particular project, you will find it in the project instructions. For example, if a project calls for multiple colors or has a choice of designs (such as Patterned Terra Cotta Pots on page 51), I might specify that you have a separate stamp for each color and/or design to make your workflow easier.

CLEANUP PRACTICES

You can continue to use your handmade stamps for many years if you clean them thoroughly and store them properly. I have stamps that I carved in college that I still use. After use, wash moldable foam block stamps gently with a damp rag. To clean purchased or carved stamps that were inked from a stamp pad, wipe the surface with a damp rag after using water-based pigment or clean with acetone (fingernail polish) if you used oil-based all-surface pigment. Allow all stamps to dry completely before storing.

Be sure to tightly close all ink pads and paint jars so they do not dry out between uses. When using acrylic craft paint for stamping, wash your stamp, brayer, and rolling surface with hot water as soon as you are done. If allowed to dry, the layers of paint are difficult to remove.

KEEP YOUR TEMPLATES

In the Stencil chapter, I recommend that you keep your used stencils and templates in a folder for future use (see page 63). You can do the same with the templates you cut out or copy for stamping as well. Inspiration can strike at any time, and having the raw materials on hand will let you get into creative mode much quicker. This will also save you time if a stamp needs to be re-carved because it was misplaced or damaged.

TIPS AND TRICKS FOR SUCCESS

Stamping should be fun and stress-free. Here are a few tips to help you achieve the results you want.

· Moldable foam blocks are very porous and they will soak up a lot of ink after being charged, so do not apply too much pressure when you are stamping.

· When you are carving the foam blocks, be sure your utility knife has a sharp blade. A dull blade causes jagged edges in the foam; a new blade will give much better results.

· A test print from a handmade stamp helps you determine if you need to tweak your carving. If you do, clean the stamp with a damp rag before you refine it.

· Save leftover material from your stamps to create new designs.

· Purchase the best set of carving tools you can afford—the better your tools are, the more successful your designs will be. Poor tools are difficult to work with, will ruin your supplies, and cause a lot of frustration.

· Bring a scrap of the material you plan to stamp on when you are shopping for paint or ink to test the color and opacity before you purchase.

You can stamp on a variety of surfaces, such as those shown here (clockwise from top center): kraft paper, silk, suede, linen, printed quilter's cotton, and canvas.

CIRCLES LINEN APRON

THIS LINEN APRON IS A GOOD EXAMPLE OF HOW A SIMPLE SHAPE CAN CREATE A VERY APPEALING PATTERN. I USED SEMI-TRANSPARENT INK TO GIVE THE ILLUSION THAT THE PATTERN HAD BEEN WOVEN INTO THE LINEN. THE SOFT BLUE COLOR ON THE NATURAL LINEN IS RELAXED AND STYLISH.

STAMP MATERIAL   Rubber carving block: 4" x 5½" (10.2 x 14 cm)

SURFACE & SUPPLIES

Linen apron

Permanent ink pad for use on fabric in the color of your choice (I used a Yellow Owl Workshop pad in Blue)

A scrap of linen or cotton, at least 8" (20.3 cm) square

Iron

Stamping kit (see page 20)

Design template on page 135

NOTE: This design would also work well on a cotton or canvas apron, but I must say that I am very partial to the way the linen took the semi-transparent ink, giving it a lovely watercolor quality.

| A. Carve the stamp | B. Charge stamp and print left to right | C. Offset each row |

PREPARE TO PRINT

1. Wash and dry the apron and then press with steam at the highest temperature to remove wrinkles.

2. Transfer the template to the rubber stamp material (see page 22). Using a utility blade, cut around the perimeter of the design and then remove the inner circle so you are left with a donut shape. Set aside the unused rubber block scraps for another project. **(A)**

3. Make test prints (see page 23) on the scrap of fabric until you are comfortable printing the stamp and the color is even.

ADD THE PATTERN AND FINISH

4. Lay your apron flat on your work surface and make sure that the ties are not under the body of the apron—this would interfere with the stamping process.

5. Charge your stamp with ink (see page 23) and begin printing at the upper left-hand corner of the apron, working left to right and re-inking the stamp in between each impression. The circles should almost be touching as you print them across the apron. **(B)**

6. Offset the second row of printing so you create an allover pattern rather than distinct rows; keep printing out past the edge of the apron, using a piece of paper under it to catch any extra ink. **(C)** Continue printing from left to right until you have covered the apron in pattern.

7. When you have stamped the entire surface, allow the ink to dry and then heat-set according to manufacturer's instructions.

> **HINT:** When you are stamping an area on a garment such as a pocket, a flat-fell seam, or a hem, the overlapped layers of the fabric will pick up more ink than a single layer. Adjust the pressure on the stamp when it covers these areas, pressing with your fingertips to get a clean even print on every layer.

COZY BEACH TOWELS

THESE BIG, COMFY BEACH TOWELS ARE A FUN SUMMER PROJECT AND WOULD LOOK GREAT PRINTED IN JUST ABOUT ANY COLOR SCHEME YOU CAN IMAGINE. WHEN IT COMES TO BEACH TOWELS, BIGGER IS DEFINITELY BETTER, SO I SUGGEST EXTRA-LARGE TERRY CLOTH TOWELS FOR STAMPING. LOOK FOR TOWELS WITHOUT RIBBING OR TEXTURAL PATTERNS SO YOU GET THE CLEANEST, MOST EVEN RESULTS.

STAMP MATERIAL Moldable foam stamp: 2 blocks, each 3" x 4" (7.6 x 10.2 cm)

SURFACE & SUPPLIES

White terry cloth beach towels (I printed 4 towels)

Textile paint in two colors of your choice (I used 2 jars of Jacquard Textile Color in Sky Blue and 1 jar in White)

2 brayers, each 1½" (3.8 cm)

1 hand towel for test printing

Iron

Stamping kit (see page 20)

Design template on page 139

PREPARE TO PRINT

1. Machine wash and dry the towels.

2. Trace over the template on page 139 and then cut out the pattern. Use a utility knife to trace around the edge, leaving an impression in the soft foam. Remove the paper template and store it in your design folder to use for another project. (A)

3. Use the utility knife to cut around the tracing of the shape with an up-and-down sawing motion, peeling back the foam as you work until you have cut all the way through the foam block. Repeat steps 2 and 3 with the second foam block so you have two identical stamps.

4. For this project I used two shades of blue, one directly from the jar and one mixed with white. Shake the jars of textile paint well and put several spoonfuls of white textile paint into a plastic cup and begin adding blue one spoonful at a time until you have your desired shade of light blue; I used approximately 3 spoonfuls of blue and one spoonful of white. Stir the paint well so that there are no streaks of white when you print.

5. Make a test print as described on page 23, using the hand towel. Lower the stamp slowly onto your test fabric so that it touches down evenly. Press down on the back of the stamp using the palm of your hand and apply even pressure over the entire surface of the stamp. Continue test printing until you have even, consistent prints.

6. When you have the desired results, repeat the process with the second color and brayer.

A. Carve the stamp

B. Print across width of towel

C. Alternate hues

ADD THE PATTERN AND FINISH

7. You will be printing across the towels from left to right. Lay out the towel flat on your work surface and smooth out any wrinkles. Starting at the top left corner of the towel, make your first print with darker blue ink, approximately 1" (2.5 cm) from the top and side edge of the towel. Lift the stamp straight up and set aside.

8. Charge the second stamp with lighter blue ink and print approximately 1" (2.5 cm) from the first stamp. Continue alternating colors as you print across the width of the towel. **(B)**

9. Reverse the order of colors for each subsequent row so that the blues alternate in a checkerboard pattern. Continue printing, alternating between light and dark blue, until you have stamped the entire towel. **(C)**

10. Repeat steps 7–9 for any remaining towels.

11. Heat-set your towels according to manufacturer's instructions.

CROSSHATCH ZIPPERED POUCH

THIS STAMPED SUEDE BAG IS THE PERFECT MARRIAGE OF LUXURY AND FUNCTION. I MADE IT FAIRLY LARGE, BUT FEEL FREE TO ADJUST THE SIZE TO ACCOMMODATE YOUR NEEDS. I FELL IN LOVE WITH THIS ROSY RED LEATHER AND STAMPING ON IT WAS A DREAM.

STAMP MATERIAL   Rubber carving block: 3" x 4" (7.6 x 10.2 cm)

SURFACE & SUPPLIES

2 pieces thin leather, each at least 13" x 8" (33 x 20.3 cm), plus a bit extra for test printing

Permanent ink pad for use on leather in the color of your choice (I used a StazOn pad in Jet Black)

Sewing machine and related supplies, including matching thread and a leather needle

¼" (6 mm) double-sided transparent sewing tape

12" (30.5 cm) brass zipper

Stamping kit (see page 20)

Design template on page 135

NOTE: The leather you buy should be very thin—it should feel almost like cloth. Any good leather store—or large fabric store—will probably have supple, easy-to-sew suede in stock. Leather is often sold by the hide and could have irregular edges. Bring a piece of paper cut to the size of your pouch when you shop so you can see if the piece of leather you are considering is going to be large enough for the project. Leather stores usually have amazing scrap bins, so do not forget to check them for one-of-a-kind pieces; you may find discontinued colors at a deep discount.

PREPARE TO PRINT

1. Transfer the design to the rubber carving block as directed on page 22.

2. Place the block on your cutting mat. Using a ruler and a utility knife, cut the design out of the rubber block, leaving the middle intact. Use a linoleum-carving tool with a V-shaped blade and carefully cut away the middle of the design, making sure that all of the rubber has been removed to leave a clean square. (If you need a refresher on carving, see page 22; remember to always cut away from your body.)

3. Make a test print as described on page 23; for this particular project, I suggest printing onto a piece of paper first to make sure it looks the way you want it to and then moving onto a scrap of suede. Continue making test prints until you find the right ratio of ink and pressure and are happy with the results.

ADD THE PATTERN

4. Trim each piece of leather so it is 13" x 8" (33 x 20.3 cm). Stamp the pattern from left to right, starting close to the upper left corner of your suede. Leave about 1" (2.5 cm) of space between each stamp. If the final stamp in your row hangs over the edge of the suede, use a piece of paper under it to catch any extra ink. This technique will give the suede the look of being covered in a continuous pattern.

A. Offset rows of pattern

5. Offset the second row of stamping below the first and begin with the stamp centered on the edge of the leather. Continue printing left to right with 1" (2.5 cm) between each print so that the pattern is staggered. Repeat this process on both pieces of suede until each is covered in an allover pattern, allowing the first side to dry before proceeding to the next. **(A)**

COMPLETE THE PROJECT

6. Turn one piece of leather over so the unprinted side is facing up. Take a piece of sewing tape and run it along the top edge of the long side of the leather. Peel away the paper backing from the sewing tape and fold the leather over approximately ⅓" (8 mm) and press it in place firmly with your fingers. Repeat to apply sewing tape on the second piece of leather.

7. Apply another strip of sewing tape onto each fold. This application of tape will keep the zipper secure when you install it, since you cannot pin the leather without leaving holes. It is best to leave the paper backing in place until you are ready to install the zipper. **(B)**

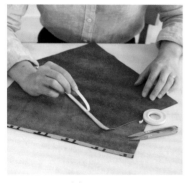

B. Add sewing tape
to folded edge

C. Stitch zipper in place

8. Put the leather needle in your sewing machine and attach a zipper foot. Place the zipper flat onto your work surface with the pull at the top. Peel away the backing from the sewing tape and place the leather on one side of the zipper tape, approximately ⅛" (3 mm) away from the zipper teeth. Use your fingers to press into place.

9. Move your needle so it is near the fold and sew the zipper in place, working from the top down. Sew as close to the fold as you are able. When you reach the bottom of the zipper, backstitch to secure.

10. Rotate the zipper unit 180° and apply the second piece of leather to the exposed zipper tape as in step 8. Stitch this side of the zipper in place, sliding the pull as needed to sew close to the fold. **(C)**

11. Unzip the zipper halfway down and fold the pouch in half with the stamped sides together. Replace the zipper foot with your normal sewing foot and move the needle back to the center position. Stitch slowly around all unfinished sides of the pouch using a ½" (1.3 cm) seam allowance, holding the pieces together with your fingertips as you go. (The suede is not slippery, so if you take your time you should have no trouble.) Be careful not to sew over the brass teeth of the zipper—it will break your needle.

12. You can add a gusset to the bag if you wish. After you have sewn all the sides together, open the zipper fully. Line up the seams in one corner so they form a neat triangle. Measure 1" (2.5 cm) from the point of the triangle and mark a line across the suede. Sew across the line. Repeat this step at the other corner of the pouch.

13. Turn your pouch right-side out and zip closed. Cut a ¼" x 6" (6 mm x 15.2 cm) piece of suede and tie it onto the end of your zipper pull for a decorative tassel.

GEOMETRIC
THROW PILLOWS

BRIGHT, GRAPHIC THROW PILLOWS ARE A FAST WAY TO ADD COLOR AND PATTERN TO A ROOM. WHILE THESE ENVELOPE-CLOSURE PILLOWS ARE ALREADY EASY TO PRINT AND SEW IN AN AFTERNOON, YOU COULD MAKE THIS PROJECT MORE QUICKLY BY PURCHASING BLANK PILLOW COVERS RATHER THAN SEWING YOUR OWN.

STAMP MATERIAL   Moldable foam stamp: 2 blocks, each 3" x 4" (7.6 x 10.2 cm)

SURFACE & SUPPLIES

1 yard (91.5 cm) natural linen, at least 44" (1.1 m) wide

All-surface acrylic paint in the colors of your choice (I used Martha Stewart Multi-Surface Satin Acrylic Craft Paint in Geranium, Beetle Black, Rubber Ducky, and Diving Board)

1½" (3.8 cm) brayer

1 yard (91.5 cm) cotton fabric for the backing

2 pillow inserts, 1 insert 16" x 26" (40.6 x 66 cm) and 1 insert 20" x 20" (50.8 x 50.8 cm)

Sewing machine and related supplies, including matching thread

Iron

Stamping kit (see page 20)

Design template on page 138

NOTE: The fabric yardage recommended for this project is enough to make two pillow covers: one 16" x 26" (40.6 x 66 cm) pillow cover and one 20" x 20" (50.8 x 50.8 cm) pillow cover, with extra fabric remaining for test printing. Feel free to make the pillows in any size or shape that you prefer. I like to use contrasting fabric on the back of my pillows for an extra dose of color and pattern.

PREPARE TO PRINT

1. Cut one 17" x 27" (43.2 x 68.6 cm) piece of prewashed linen and one 21" x 21" (53.3 x 53.3 cm) square of prewashed linen for each pillow front you plan to print. You also need a scrap for testing your stamps and paint.

2. Cut two 17" x 19" (43.2 x 48.3 cm) pieces of prewashed cotton for the back of the rectangular pillow and cut two 21" x 15" (53.3 x 38.1 cm) pieces of prewashed cotton for the square pillow. These will form the envelope closure.

3. Trace the template on page 138 onto white paper and then cut out the trapezoidal shape. Tape the template on top of the foam block and use a pencil or the utility knife from your stamping kit to trace around the edge, leaving an impression in the foam block. Remove the paper template and store it in your design folder to use for another project.

4. Use your utility knife to cut into the foam using a sawing motion, carefully following the marked line. Gently peel back the foam as you work and continue to saw through the remaining foam until it completely separates from the block. Carve a block for each color of paint you use.

5. Make a test print as described on page 23. Continue test printing as necessary until you have even, consistent prints. Stamps made from these foam blocks do not need a heavy hand. They are quite porous and will soak up pigment, so after a few test prints they deliver smooth, even results without having to apply too much pressure.

A. Stamp from left to right   B. Rotate stamp after each row   C. Insert pillow form

ADD THE PATTERN

6. You will be working across the fabric from left to right for this project. Charge the stamp and begin printing at the upper left corner of the fabric, about 1" (2.5 cm) below the top edge, aligning one straight side of the trapezoid with the top of the linen. Lift your stamp, reapply paint, and then print again next to the first stamp, letting the two prints just touch at the edges. Continue stamping across the linen in a row until you reach the edge of your fabric. **(A)**

7. For the next row of printing, rotate your stamp 180°, turning the stamp upside down. Measure 1" (2.5 cm) down the fabric and print as you did in step 6. Continue stamping your pattern in this fashion, rotating the stamp 180° after each row until the entire surface of the linen is covered in pattern. (You can also build the pattern in the opposite orientation, by starting with the short side of the trapezoid at the top of the fabric; see the aqua pillow on page 38 for an example of the pattern created in this way.) **(B)**

8. Allow the paint to dry completely and then heat-set following the manufacturer's instructions.

COMPLETE THE PROJECT

9. Finish one short edge on each of the back pieces for the rectangular pillow and finish one long edge on each of the back pieces for the square pillow: Fold in ½" (1.3 cm) and press, fold in another ½" (1.3 cm) and press again. Stitch each edge.

10. Place each back piece on the decorated front, right sides facing, aligning the unfinished edges; one back piece will overlap the other. Pin in place and stitch all the way around using a ½"(1.3 cm) seam allowance.

11. Turn each pillow right-side out and give it a good pressing so it is flat and crisp. Open the envelope at the back of each pillow and place the pillow form inside. **(C)**

> **HINT:** If you want to use contrasting fabric for your pillow backs, small prints in neutral colors work best. Tiny polka dots, checks, or floral prints are a good bet for mixing with bold designs; I used a black-and-white pin dot pattern for this collection of pillows.

BLOOMING MARKET BAGS

THESE STURDY, LIGHTWEIGHT, FLAT-BOTTOMED MUSLIN BAGS ARE PERFECT FOR HOLDING ANYTHING FROM LOOSE GRAINS TO PRODUCE. CHOOSE FROM THE SIX FLORAL DESIGNS I'VE PROVIDED OR DESIGN YOUR OWN, THEN GET STARTED ON THIS EASY AFTERNOON PROJECT.

STAMP MATERIAL   Rubber carving block: 11¾" x 11¾" (30 x 30 cm)

SURFACE & SUPPLIES

2 yards (1.8 m) unbleached 100% cotton muslin, at least 44" (1.1 m) wide

Permanent ink pads for use on fabric, in the colors of your choice (I used Yellow Owl Workshop pads in Brown, Green, Red, Blue, and Orange)

3½ yards (3.2 m) cotton cord

Sewing machine and related supplies, including matching thread

Iron

Stamping kit (see page 20)

Design templates on page 140

NOTE: There are enough materials listed to make 3 market bags: 2 small bags (approximately 5½" x 10" [14 x 25.4 cm]) and 1 large bag (approximately 9" x 13½" [22.9 x 34.3 cm])

PREPARE TO PRINT

1. Transfer the designs as directed on page 22; all the designs will fit on a large carving block and you can cut them away to form separate stamps. Make sure to also trace the lines at the edge of each petal, as these are part of the perimeter of the stamp. **(A)**

2. Carve the block as described on page 22. Use a linoleum-carving tool with a small V-shaped blade. Hold the tool in your hand with the end resting in your palm and the V shape facing up; slowly carve away from your body, applying even pressure to the cutter. Cut away all the material except the transferred design, which will be in relief. Repeat this step to carve as many of the designs as you would like. **(B)**

3. Cut out all the bag pieces from prewashed muslin: for a small bag, cut 1 rectangle that is 12½" x 15" (31.8 x 38.1 cm) and 1 round bottom piece that is 5" (12.7 cm) in diameter; for a large bag, cut 1 rectangle that is 16" x 22" (40.6 x 55.9 cm) and 1 round bottom piece that is 8" (20.3 cm) in diameter. Press the pieces with an iron in preparation for stamping.

4. Make a test print (see page 23) on swatches of the leftover muslin. **(C)**

A. Transfer the design to the carving block

B. Carve the stamp

C. Make test prints

ADD THE PATTERN

5. Print from left to right, beginning at the top left-hand corner. Place the edge of the stamp at the edge of the fabric and stamp the designs as you did your test prints. Continue printing in rows until the entire surface is covered in pattern.

6. Repeat step 5 on all pattern pieces—and do not forget the circular bottom pieces! Let all ink dry completely and follow the manufacturer's recommendations to heat-set.

D. Baste and gather edges of the bottom piece

E. Stitch right sides together to create the bag

F. Pin and attach the bottom piece

COMPLETE THE PROJECT

7. Stitch a row of wide basting stitches around each bottom piece, about ¼" (6 mm) from the edge. Pull the threads to pucker the bottom piece slightly; the lip that forms will help you pin the bottom in place. **(D)**

8. You will construct each bag by folding a fabric rectangle in half and sewing it along the open side. Begin by making a narrow hem along each shorter edge of the fabric rectangle that corresponds to the bag you wish to make—the 12½" (31.8 cm) sides for a smaller bag and the 16" (40.6 cm) sides for a longer bag. At each side, turn in ½" (1.3 cm) and press, then fold in another ½" (1.3 cm) and stitch in place.

9. Make a tunnel for the drawstring along one unfinished edge of the piece used in step 8. Fold the edge down 1" (2.5 cm) and press, and fold down another 1" (2.5 cm) and press. Stitch along the first folded edge to form the tunnel. This will be the top of the bag.

10. Fold the rectangle in half with right sides together, hemmed side edges aligned. Pin in place and stitch using a ½" (1.3 cm) seam allowance. Sew as close as you can to the tunnel, but do not sew it shut. Backstitch to secure the seam. Leave the bag inside out. **(E)**

11. With right sides together, pin the bottom piece to the bag, adjusting the basting stitches to fit if needed. Stitch the bottom to the bag using a ½" (1.3 cm) seam allowance. **(F)**

12. Attach a safety pin to the end of the cotton cord and push it through the tunnel, leaving about 6" (15.2 cm) free on either side of the bag. Trim the cord and tie a knot at the end. When you need to wash the bags, do so by hand and let them air dry.

HINT: Test prints will show you if you need to refine the carving; sometimes there may be a spot on the stamp you forgot to carve away. Gently clean the surface of the stamp before you make any corrections.

VARIATION: DAISY PRINT TOTE BAG

This canvas tote bag is a charming project that shows how adaptable your hand-carved stamps can be. I repurposed my favorite floral stamp from the Blooming Market Bags (page 42) to print a cheerful pattern onto a basic blank tote. Instead of, or in addition to, stitching your own muslin bags, you can make this project with a plain premade canvas tote bag. These inexpensive bags are easily found at craft and art stores and are invaluable for trips to the market or library—and of course they are great for toting children's items. Keep a supply in the car so you always have one on hand.

STAMP MATERIAL   Rubber carving block: 11¾" x 11¾" (30 cm x 30 cm)

SURFACE & SUPPLIES

Blank cotton tote bag

Permanent ink pad for use on fabric, in the color of your choice (I used a Yellow Owl Workshop pad in Red)

Scrap canvas or old tote for test printing

Iron

Stamping kit (see page 20)

PREPARE TO PRINT

1. Iron your tote to remove all wrinkles. Prepare the stamp you created for the Blooming Market Bags, or carve a new design following the instructions in steps 1–2 on page 44.

2. Make a test print or two on your scrap canvas. I suggest marking the back of the stamp with an arrow facing up so you can change the orientation of the stamp as you print, giving the pattern a more organic look and feel. **(A)**

| A. Mark the stamp | B. Print in offset rows | C. Cover the entire surface and let dry |

ADD THE PATTERN AND FINISH

3. Spread the tote bag out flat on your work surface and smooth away any wrinkles. Charge your stamp and starting at the upper left corner, print in loose offset rows, rotating the stamp in between prints. **(B)**

4. Continue stamping from left to right until you have covered the entire surface of the tote bag. **(C)** Allow the ink to dry and repeat on the other side of the bag if desired. When the ink is dry, heat-set according to the manufacturer's instructions.

HANDMADE
WRAPPING PAPER

HAND-PRINTED WRAPPING PAPER MAKES THE GIFT INSIDE EVEN MORE MEANINGFUL. THE PATTERNS FOR THIS PROJECT ARE SO STRAIGHTFOR-WARD THAT I INVITE YOU TO HAVE FUN PLAYING WITH THE COLORS AND PLACEMENT OF THE SHAPES. THIS TECHNIQUE COULD EASILY BE ADAPTED FOR OTHER PAPER PROJECTS, SUCH AS GIFT BAGS, NOTE CARDS, OR PAR-TY DÉCOR. IF YOU LIKE TO SPEND TIME CRAFTING WITH YOUR CHILDREN, THIS PROJECT IS IDEAL. ANY PATTERN LOOKS LOVELY WHEN STAMPED BY LITTLE HANDS, NO MATTER HOW "MESSY."

STAMP MATERIAL Moldable foam stamp: 4 blocks, each 3" x 4" (7.6 x 10.2 cm)

SURFACE & SUPPLIES

1 roll kraft paper, 30" x 10' (76.2 cm x 3 m)

All-surface acrylic paint in the colors of your choice (I used Martha Stewart Multi-Surface Satin Acrylic Craft Paint in Geranium, Amaranth, Scottish Highlands, Vanilla Bean, and Indigo)

1½" (3.8 cm) brayer

Stamping kit (see page 20)

Design templates on page 138

NOTE: Kraft paper is sold under various names, including postal wrap or butcher paper. The 30" x 10' (76.2 cm x 3 m) roll specified in the instructions will make 5 sheets of wrapping paper, each 30" x 24" (76.2 x 61 cm).

PREPARE TO PRINT

1. Cut the roll of paper into 30" x 24" (76.2 x 61 cm) sheets. Do not worry if the paper curls up—the moisture from the paint will help flatten the sheets after you have finished printing.

2. Trace the templates on page 138 and then cut out the shapes you want to use. Tape each template on top of the foam block and use an utility knife to trace around the edge, leaving an impression in the soft foam. **(A)**

3. Use the utility knife to cut into the foam using a sawing motion, carefully following the traced line. Gently peel back foam as you work and continue to saw through the remaining foam until it separates fully. Repeat steps 2 and 3 to carve as many of the designs as you would like, placing a separate design on each block.

4. Make a test print as described on page 23. Continue test printing as needed.

A. Carve each stamp   B. Secure the paper   C. Print in vertical stripes

ADD THE PATTERN AND FINISH

5. Take one of the sheets of paper and tape all four corners to your work surface to keep it flat while you print. **(B)**

6. Choose your first stamp and charge with paint as you did when making the test prints. Print in vertical stripes from left to right until the entire sheet of paper is covered with pattern, leaving at least 1" (2.5 cm) between each stripe. (See the photo on page 48 for pattern placement ideas.) **(C)**

7. Repeat steps 5 and 6 for each stamp and color you decide to use for the wrapping paper. Be sure to clean and dry your stamp and brayer in between paint colors as needed.

8. Lay the sheets of paper flat to dry; store rolled or flat.

HINT: Because the foam stamp block material will absorb lots of ink, you can often print two or three times on paper before having to reapply paint with the brayer.

PATTERNED TERRA COTTA POTS

ADDING YOUR OWN COLOR AND PATTERN IS AN EASY WAY TO FRESHEN UP AND PERSONALIZE PLAIN TERRA COTTA PLANTERS. IF YOU USE AN ALL-SURFACE ACRYLIC PAINT, YOU HAVE THE OPTION OF USING THE PLANTERS INDOORS OR OUT.

STAMP MATERIAL   Moldable foam stamp: 3 blocks, each 3" x 4" (7.6 x 10.2 cm)

SURFACE & SUPPLIES

Terra cotta pots in various sizes

All-surface acrylic paint in the colors of your choice (I used Martha Stewart Multi-Surface Satin Acrylic Craft Paint in Amaranth, Porcelain Doll, Chipotle, Vanilla Bean, Pond, Indigo, Japanese Maple, and Geranium)

1½" (3.8 cm) brayer

1 old pot for test printing

Stamping kit (see page 20)

Design templates on page 138

PREPARE TO PRINT

1. Use a slightly damp rag to remove any dirt or dust from the surface of your pots and set them aside to dry.

2. Trace the templates on page 138 onto white paper, cut out the shapes, and tape them on top of a foam stamp block. To make the most efficient use of the material, you can put multiple designs on each block and then cut the block into separate stamps.

3. Use a pencil to trace around the edge of the shapes, which will leave an impression in the soft foam. Use a utility knife to carefully follow the pencil line and cut into the foam using an up-and-down sawing motion; you can get a nice clean line using a ruler as a guide. Gently peel back the foam and continue to saw through it until the foam separates fully. Repeat steps 2 and 3 to make as many stamps as you would like. **(A)**

4. Make a test print on an old pot as described on page 23.

A. Cut the stamps

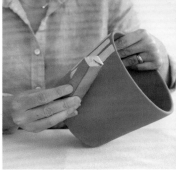

B. Create the pattern

C. Overlap designs and play with color

ADD THE PATTERN AND FINISH

5. Use the brayer to roll ink onto the surface of the stamp and make your first print just under the top lip of the pot. Starting at the top edge helps you keep your pattern even as you move down the surface. Hold the stamp so it comes down flat onto the surface of the pot. Gently rock it if needed so the inked surface of the stamp makes full contact with the curved sides of the pot. **(B)**

6. Charge your stamp in between prints. See the photos below and on page 51 as inspiration for decorating your pots; overlap designs and play with the color combinations as desired. **(C)**

7. After cleaning up your materials (page 24), allow the paint to fully dry before using the pots.

> **HINT:** I like using the moldable foam blocks for this project because they are pliable. This quality makes it easier to get a clean print on a round pot because you can bend the stamp slightly to make good contact with the surface.

STENCIL

STENCILING BASICS

STENCILS ARE WONDERFUL DESIGN TOOLS AS THEY ARE INCREDIBLY VERSATILE, WHETHER HAND-CUT OR PREMADE AND PURCHASED. THEY CAN LEND BEAUTIFUL CHARACTER TO YOUR HOME AND WARDROBE, EITHER THROUGH A SINGLE IMAGE (AN INDIVIDUAL MOTIF) OR THROUGH A PATTERN (A GROUP OF REPEATED IMAGES). IN THIS CHAPTER I EXPLORE THE FULL RANGE OF POSSIBILITIES THAT STENCILS OFFER, FROM LUSH FLORALS AND FOLK-ART MOTIFS TO CLEAN GEOMETRIC DESIGNS. WITH THE RIGHT TOOLS AND A BIT OF INSTRUCTION, STENCILS MAKE IT POSSIBLE TO DECO-RATE ALMOST ANYTHING YOUR HEART DESIRES, FROM TEXTILES TO CERAMICS TO FURNITURE.

ANATOMY OF A STENCIL

Stencils are among the oldest and most popular surface design tools, and for good reason—they are simple to make and easy to use. Stencils are made from an impervious material such as paper, cardboard, or plastic film that acts as a resist to paint or pigment. The design is cut away from the solid material—the resist—to make the stencil. Paint is applied through the design, creating a pattern on the surface below. You can create clean, line-based patterns like stripes or grids using very simple stencils made from repositionable tape, or you can make an intricate hand-cut design.

I enjoy cutting my own stencils to create designs that are truly unique, but I also find value in working with commercial stencils for certain projects. For example, if I want a precise all-over geometric pattern, I turn to machine-cut drafting stencils, which are sold in a large array of shapes and sizes in most art supply stores.

A LONG, COLORFUL HISTORY
Stencils have been used to decorate since prehistoric times, when Paleolithic people made images on cave walls. Stencils decorated tombs in Egypt, walls in Pompeii, and signs in Rome.

WORKING WITH MULTIPLE COLORS

When using a stencil, it is easy to design with more than one color. You can cut multiple stencils, one for each color, and then layer them, or you can create beautiful multicolored designs with a single stencil, which is the method I chose for the projects in this chapter.

STENCIL SUPPLIES AND TOOLS

ADHESIVE STENCIL FILM
Adhesive-backed stencil film is semi-transparent, pliable plastic with a removable paper backing; it comes on a roll. The adhesive on the back is strong enough to keep it in place and reuse, yet does not leave any sticky residue on your project. It is also supple enough to use on curved or uneven surfaces, which comes in handy for stenciling on dimensional surfaces, such as the lamp on page 74.

STENCILING TOOLS AND MATERIALS:
1. Contact paper 2. Adhesive stencil film 3. Stencil film blank 4. Utility knife 5 and 6. Paper backing from adhesive stencil film

Since this film is semi-transparent, it is ideal for stencil projects that call for layering colors or images; you can see through the film to ensure proper placement of your design. The paper backing also has a grid, which is helpful for placing images, and it cuts easily with a utility knife and scissors. I have had great results using the Martha Stewart Adhesive Stencil Film, sold at major craft chains; a roll is 11 inches (27.9 cm) wide x 3 yards (2.7 m) long.

STENCIL FILM BLANKS

Medium-weight clear plastic film (often sold under its brand name Mylar in art supply stores) is another great material for stenciling. Unlike the adhesive stencil film, however, the film blanks are best suited for use on flat surfaces because they will not bend. If needed, you use repositionable adhesive spray to secure this material in place while you are working.

The plastic is transparent, perfect for tracing over existing designs. I am fond of the blue-tinted blanks because they provide contrast when I am working on a light surface. My favorite product is Grafix Blue Stencil Film, available in 9 x 12-inch (22.9 x 30.5 cm) sheets; there are four sheets in each package. These blanks are available online, but most art supply stores have a similar product. Mylar is also available in larger sizes if you are working at a grander scale.

Because these sheets are thicker and sturdier than other resists they are less likely to tear, and they are easy to clean and reuse for multiple projects. Although they are stiff, they cut easily with a utility knife.

OTHER RESIST MATERIALS

Other materials that can be used as resists are contact paper (which I chose for the Modern Side Chair on page 77) and artist tape (which worked wonderfully for the Striped Storage Basket on page 90).

PAINT AND PIGMENT

For most of the projects in this chapter I use versatile acrylic paints that can be applied to multiple surfaces. Read about them in more detail in Getting Started on page 13.

Textile paints have specific qualities that make them appropriate for use on fabric. They leave the textiles with a soft hand because the pigment is not stiff when it dries. This is especially important when you are working on home textiles, where comfort is a factor. Learn more about textile paint on page 13.

REPOSITIONABLE ADHESIVE SPRAY

Repositionable adhesive spray is sprayed onto the back of stencil film blanks to secure them to your surface and keep the edges flush while you are applying paint (keeping the pigment from bleeding under the stencil lines). It provides secure hold without leaving your project surface sticky.

ARTIST TRANSFER PAPER

Artist transfer paper comes in 8½ x 11-inch (21.6 x 27.9 cm) sheets. It is used for transferring the design templates onto the repositionable stencil film that is used for many of projects in this chapter. The transfer paper is reusable and can be folded and stored when not in use; you can use it to transfer your own artwork, too, if you would like to substitute one of your designs for any of the projects.

STENCIL BRUSHES

It is good to have a variety of brushes on hand when you are printing. Traditional stencil brushes are cylindrical with a round flat top and are most commonly made from coarse, rigid natural-fiber bristles. Stencil brushes are used differently from a paintbrush, which is stroked across a surface; they are designed to tap paint through the stencil in a technique called stippling (page 62). Stippling ensures a clean print by keeping paint from bleeding under the edges of the design.

Stencil brushes are inexpensive and are often packaged in a set of three, with a small, medium, and large brush included in each set. Choose a brush that is a bit wider than the design you are printing so it does not disturb the edges. I find that the ½-inch (1.3 cm) diameter stencil brushes are the most versatile. Stencil brushes can be washed and reused for many projects before having to be replaced. I like to use them for larger projects, especially those on canvas or coarsely woven materials, because they can deliver a lot of pigment to a surface that has texture. You can find stencil brushes in any well-stocked art or craft store.

PIGMENT AND TOOLS:

1. All-surface acrylic paint 2. Stencil brush 3. Foam daubers
4. Acrylic artist palette 5. Plastic spoons and cups 6. Stencil-printed cotton fabric

FOAM DAUBERS

For smaller projects, I prefer foam daubers, sometimes called dabbers. Daubers have plastic handles and a flat circular top made of high-quality foam. They are often sold in sets that include multiple sizes, generally from ¼ inch to ¾ inch (6 mm to 1.9 cm). Daubers offer consistent, even paint delivery from the foam top and are used in the same way as a traditional stencil brush.

Daubers can provide an almost airbrush-like quality when they are applying paint, similar to a high-end cosmetics sponge. They are best suited for projects with fine details and very smooth surfaces such as ceramics; they are generally good for several small projects before needing to be replaced. The sets are inexpensive and they are great for multiple color designs; keep a couple of sets on hand so you have a separate dauber for each color in your project. This is efficient because you do not have to take the time to wash your dauber between colors—the foam will become saturated with water while being washed and then must dry out before you can use it again. Having separate daubers for a multiple-color stencil design also eliminates the risk of having your paint contaminated by another color.

Traditional stencil brushes are more coarse and dry and require a little bit more paint, making them better suited for those absorbent surfaces such as thick fabric or wicker. The foam daubers will hold a more even layer of pigment than a brush, requiring a lighter hand as you print. Daubers are available at art and craft stores and can be purchased online.

FOAM PAINT ROLLER

This applicator is well suited for the reverse stencil technique I used for the Modern Side Chair on page 77, where the design on the chair back is painted rather than stippled through a stencil.

POSITIVE OR NEGATIVE?

When you become adept at using stencils, you will probably want to incorporate your own designs. It is important to remember the principles of positive and negative space when you are cutting your stencils; any areas that you cut out of the stencil medium will print as positive space.

CUTTING TOOLS

A precision utility knife will allow you to "draw" around shapes in a fluid motion (see page 61). A pair of sharp scissors is also invaluable. I find that for cutting away large areas from a stencil—especially ones with lots of curved edges—I prefer using scissors to a utility knife. Experiment with each to find which tool works best for you.

You will also use your self-healing cutting mat quite often. Buy the largest mat that will fit on your primary work surface. Self-healing mats can work double-duty as a cutting surface while also protecting your work area from paint and water.

MAKING AND USING STENCILS

Though the projects in this chapter offer a lot of variety, there are some basic techniques that apply to almost all of them. You will make most of the stencils from either adhesive stencil film or a stencil film blank; both methods are described below.

PREPARE THE WORK AREA

Because you will be working with paint, ink, or other types of pigment, be sure to protect your work surface with a length of canvas or a drop cloth; the latter works well for larger projects. (Newspaper or kraft paper can be used in a pinch, but canvas provides a better printing surface and can be reused for multiple projects.) Assemble your tools before you begin so you can work without distractions.

PREPARE THE PRINTING SURFACE

If you are working with fabric other than canvas, wash, dry, and iron to prep it. If you are working on another surface, such as metal or wood (including manufactured items like a lamp or chair), use a clean, damp cloth to wipe away any dirt or dust from the surface and let it dry completely before you begin to print.

TRANSFER THE DESIGN

If using adhesive stencil film, photocopy the design onto a standard sheet of 8½ x 11-inch (21.6 x 27.9 cm) paper. Using scissors or a utility knife, cut a piece of adhesive-backed film to the same dimensions as the photocopy. Gently tape the transfer paper (pigment-side up) to your cutting mat. Place your stencil film (paper-side down) on top of the transfer paper and tape into place; tape your photocopied design on top so that

the stencil film is sandwiched between the transfer paper and the templates. **(A)**

Trace around the perimeter of the design with a sharp pencil. **(B)** Remove all of the tape from the corners of your photocopy, stencil film, and transfer paper. Set the photocopy and transfer paper aside for another use or discard.

If you are using stencil film blanks, you will not need the transfer paper. Simply place the transparent sheet over the photocopied design template and trace around the motif with a fine-point permanent marker.

CUT THE STENCIL

Tape the stencil to your cutting surface with the design facing you—this will be either the paper backing on the stencil film or the tracing made with a permanent marker on the plastic sheet. Hold the utility knife as you would a pencil and cut along the edges of the transferred design. **(C)** As the cut pieces come loose, you can discard them. Make sure to cut using clean, fluid lines so the edges of your stencil are crisp, and replace the blade in your utility knife often. Use scissors

to trim down the stencil material as needed. If you can, try to leave a margin of at least a couple of inches (centimeters) around the perimeter of the design to keep the ink from bleeding off onto the surface unless the directions instruct otherwise.

SECURE THE STENCIL

You must adhere the stencil carefully to your printing surface to ensure a clean, crisp print. If you are using stencil film, peel off the paper backing **(D)** and lay it flat on the surface; if you are using a stencil blank, apply repositionable spray to it and place it on the surface. Press either stencil material firmly into place, paying special attention to the inside edges of your stencil. To make sure that it is adhering well, use a bone folder, the back of a spoon, or your thumbnail to rub the edges completely flat against your surface. **(E)**

MIX CUSTOM COLORS

If you plan to use a custom color of paint, you should mix it before moving on to the next step. Read about mixing paint colors on page 14.

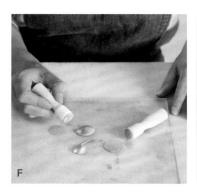

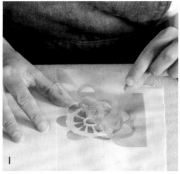

PRINT THE STENCIL

Stencil printing uses a specific technique called *loading and stippling*. Loading refers to adding paint to your brush and stippling is a method of delivering a thin, relatively dry layer of paint onto the surface through the stencil.

To load and stipple, place a small amount of paint on an artist palette—maybe a dollop the size of a quarter. Dip just the tip of your dauber or bristles into the paint. **(F)** Position the tool at a 90° angle to your palette, so its surface is flat against the palette, and tap gently to distribute the paint evenly through the foam or bristles before you print. **(G)**

The most important step when you are stenciling is having the correct amount of pigment on your applicator. Start with multiple layers of dry, even color when you begin and add more paint after you get a feel for the materials. Stipple through the stencil with gentle tapping motions until you see that the surface below is being covered in an even layer of paint, adding small amounts of pigment as necessary. **(H)** You may need to repeat this process several times since you want to add thin layers of paint at a time; be sure to tap the applicator against the palette to spread the paint each time you add a layer of color to the stencil.

The loading and stippling technique is the same no matter what type of applicator you decide to use for printing, but do take some time to get the feel for each kind of tool used in this chapter before you begin printing. When using multiple colors on a single project, it is best to have a separate applicator for each color. **(I)**

MAKE A TEST PRINT

Before you actually begin a project, it is important to test print on your chosen surface if you can; it is easy to do a test print when you are working on paper or fabric and have excess material, but is not always practical if you are working on a purchased object such as a ceramic bowl. I encourage you to think outside the box, though: If you are inspired to work on a ceramic project, for example, use an old plate or platter for test printing. You can use it over and over again as long as you have free surface area!

To create a template that you can use for test printing, take a piece of stencil material that is roughly 4 x 6 inches (10.2 x 15.2 cm)—a large scrap will also do—and use the utility blade to cut out a few small shapes of your choice. **(J)**

Peel off the paper backing from the stencil film or apply repositionable spray to the stencil film blank and place it flat on your surface. Use your fingertips to press it in place securely and remove any air bubbles, paying particular attention to the inside edges of the stencil. Apply the paint using the load-and-stipple technique described at left.

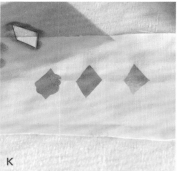

When the paint on the test print is dry, carefully pull the stencil off and examine your work. **(K)** If there are pools of paint on the edges of the design, you may not have pressed the stencil into the surface properly or you used too much paint, which caused flooding under the stencil. If your paint is too light, you can experiment with adding a tiny bit more to your brush when you're loading it. Alternatively, you can try adding another layer of paint.

PRINT THE PROJECTS

The basic techniques you need to make the stencil projects are outlined in this section, and you will be referred back to this information in each set of instructions as appropriate. Any project-specific information—such as where to begin stenciling—is included there as well as any directions for creating custom colors. When you are working on a purchased item, such as the Playful Ceramic Platters on page 86, your item may not be exactly the same dimensions as mine, so you will need to plan the spacing of your design. Compare it to my project to get a general sense of the proportion of the pattern.

CLEANUP PRACTICES

Wash the applicators and other tools in cool water until it runs clear and allow them to dry completely. If you have pigment left over, save in a small jar for another use or discard safely.

SPECIAL TECHNIQUES—REVERSE STENCILING

This technique provides a twist on the typical process; for a reverse stencil, you cut the design element out of the stencil material and the motif itself serves as the resist. Pigment is applied over it, revealing the original surface when the stencil is peeled away. See this technique in the Modern Side Chair project on page 77. **(L)**

KEEP YOUR STENCILS!

The stencils that you create with care will become an invaluable visual library for future projects; glance through them every now and then when you are in a creative mood. I suggest keeping all of your stencils (including the paper backing or photocopies of a template) in a folder for reference. If the stencils have an adhesive backing on them, store them in between sheets of wax paper. Having designs on hand and ready to go makes spontaneous printing effortless; you never know when inspiration may strike.

A STENCIL FOR EVERY SURFACE

The versatility of stencils can't be underestimated; all you have to do is glance through the variety of surfaces, or substrates, that I use in the book to see just how many different ways they can be used. Stencils decorate equally well on fabric, paper, metal, leather, wood, and ceramics, and can be applied to furniture and walls, too. A simple test print (see page 62) can quickly let you know if the surface is suitable.

STENCILING KIT

Each set of project instructions includes a list of specific supplies, but there are a number of basic items that you will need for practically every stenciling project. Arrange them nearby when you begin working; organization at the beginning of a project frees you to focus your energies on the creative process.

· Canvas drop cloth

· Utility knife with extra blades

· Scissors

· Self-healing cutting mat

· Sharp pencil and fine-point permanent marker

· Ruler and/or yardstick

· Plastic or paper cups for mixing ink

· Plastic spoons

· Acrylic artist palette

· Artist transfer paper

· Artist tape

· Scrap paper

· Cotton balls and/or swabs

· ¼-inch (6 mm) fine-tipped paintbrushes for touch-ups

TIPS AND TRICKS FOR SUCCESS

As with most endeavors, your stenciling technique will improve with practice. Although I have mentioned all these tips before, it is important to keep them in mind as you work so you will have success with your stenciling, starting with your very first project.

· Stencils work best on smooth, clean surfaces. Take the time to clean your surface (especially a wood or ceramic object) and let it dry completely before you begin your project.

· Make sure the edge of your stencil is completely flat against your project surface. The inside edges of your stencils need to be free of any bumps or air bubbles so the pigment cannot leak underneath to the surface you are decorating. Remember to rub the edges of the stencil flush against your project surface.

· Take the time to test your technique and make sure you are loading the right amount of pigment on your applicator. Remember to load pigment to the brush's bristles only; if you are using a foam applicator, use the most even amount of pigment possible.

· Make sure that the paint is dry before you peel away your stencil. Exercising patience will ensure that wet paint will not smudge or leak, marring your work.

· Use a sharp cutting tool! Change your blades often if you are using a utility knife, especially if you are cutting through paper when making your stencil. It is easier and safer to work with a sharp blade.

STENCILING TOOLS AND MATERIALS:
1. Utility knife and extra blades 2. Acrylic artist palette
3. Newsprint 4. Adhesive stencil film (back) 5. Artist transfer paper 6. Self-healing cutting mat 7. Ruler 8. Canvas drop cloth 9. Adhesive stencil film 10. Soft lead pencil 11. Fine-point marker 12. Scissors 13. Plastic spoons and cups
14. Cotton balls 15. Foam dauber 16. White artist tape
17. Adhesive spray 18. Stencil film blank

FLORAL TOTE BAG

A RAMBLING FLORAL DESIGN, STENCILED IN TWO COLORS, ALONG WITH BEAUTIFUL LEATHER HANDLES AND SHINY BRASS HARDWARE, TAKE THIS TOTE UP A NOTCH IN THE STYLE DEPARTMENT. FOR A QUICKER VERSION, YOU CAN STENCIL A PREMADE TOTE.

STENCIL MATERIAL   Adhesive stencil film

SURFACE & SUPPLIES

¾ yard (68.6 cm) unwashed natural cotton canvas for the bag, at least 44" (1.1 m) wide

All-surface acrylic paint in 3 colors of your choice (I used Martha Stewart Multi-Surface Satin Acrylic Craft Paint in Wild Blueberry, Pink Flamingo, and Porcelain Doll)

2 foam daubers, each ½" (1.3 cm) wide

½ yard (45.7 cm) cotton for the lining, at least 44" (1.1 m) wide

½ yard (45.7 cm) medium-weight fusible interfacing

2 leather straps, each ⅝" (1.6 cm) wide x 26" (66 cm) long (available at leather stores; see Resources, page 142)

Brass rivets (available at leather stores; see Resources, page 142)

Sewing machine and related supplies, including matching thread

Iron

Leather riveting kit (optional)

Stenciling kit (see page 65)

Design templates on page 134

NOTE: My local leather store added the straps to my tote. For other options, see step 16 on page 69.

PREPARE TO PRINT

1. Transfer the designs from the templates onto stencil film as described on page 60.

2. Cut the stencils, referring to the directions on page 61 as needed.

3. Cut two 16" (40.6 cm) squares from the canvas, the cotton lining, and the fusible interfacing. Set the leftover canvas aside for test printing. Iron the fusible interfacing onto one side of each piece of canvas, following the manufacturer's instructions. (The interfacing will help give the canvas more structure for a sturdy, more attractive bag.)

4. Shake the jars of paint well before using. Make two custom blends (see page 14):
For the navy blue, use one spoonful of navy ink and half a spoonful of white and mix thoroughly.
For the pink, use one spoonful of salmon pink and half a spoonful of white and mix thoroughly.

5. Make a test print (see page 62) on the leftover canvas.

A. Secure stencil film

B. Allow ink to dry and remove stencil slowly

C. Repeat until canvas is covered

ADD THE PATTERN

6. Lay out one the squares of prepared canvas, interfacing-side down. Peel away the paper backing of the stencil. Place the smaller "bud" stencil in the top right-hand corner of the canvas, leaving a margin of at least 2" (5.1 cm) between the cut areas of the stencil and the edge of the fabric, and position the "flower" stencil slightly below and to the left. Smooth out any wrinkles with your fingers, making sure that the stencil makes full contact with the fabric. **(A)**

7. Starting with pink, begin stippling the paint into the petals of the design. Since this two-color design uses only one stencil, it is very important that you don't let pink paint travel into the center of the flower (which is to be navy blue) or onto the leaves (also to be blue). When you are satisfied with the coverage of pink paint in the petals, let the paint dry enough that it will not smudge when you move onto your next print.

8. Using a fresh dauber for the blue paint, print the centers and leaves. Allow all of the ink to dry completely and then slowly peel away the stencil film, taking extra care to make sure that it does not rip or tear. **(B)**

9. Continue printing, following the process in steps 7 and 8; use my arrangement of pattern as a guide or develop your own. I suggest rotating the stencils as you use them for an organic placement of motifs. Continue until you have covered the entire square with pattern. **(C)** Do not be concerned if the pattern does not repeat exactly. This design is meant to be loose and free.

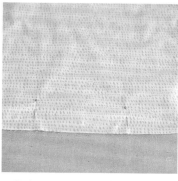

D. Pin canvas and lining pieces together

E. Leave opening for turning

F. Stitch the gusset

COMPLETE THE PROJECT

All seam allowances are ½" (1.3 cm) unless otherwise noted.

10. Take one canvas square and one lining square and place them right sides together. Pin together along the top edge and stitch. Repeat with the remaining bag and lining pieces.

11. Fold the lining open on one of the pieces so it creates a long rectangle. Repeat with the second piece and place it on top so the right sides are together; pin in place on all sides. **(D)**

12. Stitch along the edges, beginning approximately 4" (10.2 cm) from one corner of the lining; leave about 8" (20.3 cm) open in the lining for turning as shown. **(E)**

13. To make the gussets, fold one corner of the canvas bag so the side and end seams align, forming a triangle. Measure and mark a line 2" (5.1 cm) from the tip of the point; stitch across the line. **(F)** Repeat on the other corner of the canvas and along both bottom corners of the cotton lining.

14. Carefully pull the canvas through the hole in the lining. Turn the raw edges of the opening under, press if needed, and sew the opening shut with a ½" (1.3 cm) seam allowance. Make sure the corners meet and the gussets are flat inside the bottom of the bag.

15. Press the top edge of the tote and then topstitch ¼" (6 mm) around the top of the bag to keep the lining in place and give the tote a polished look.

16. Take the finished tote to a leather store and have the leather straps installed approximately 2" (5.1 cm) below the top edge of the tote. If you would prefer to install them yourself, use a leather riveting setter, brass rivets, and straps to complete your tote. Major craft or fabric chains sell rivet kits and replacement straps, as well as alternate strap materials.

BRIGHT TABLE LINENS

WHEN YOU SET A TABLE WITH BEAUTIFUL LINENS, IT MAKES ANY MEAL FEEL LIKE A SPECIAL OCCASION. IF YOU LIKE, YOU CAN ADJUST THE COLORS OF THE CRISP FLORAL DESIGN TO SUIT YOUR TABLEWEAR AND/ OR THE SEASONS.

STENCIL MATERIAL   Adhesive stencil film

SURFACE & SUPPLIES

2¾ yards (2.5 m) white medium-weight linen or cotton, at least 44" (1.1 m) wide, prewashed

Textile paints in 3 colors of your choice (I used Jacquard Textile Color in Yellow Ochre, Black, and White)

2 foam daubers, each ⅝" (1.6 cm wide)

Sewing machine and related supplies, including matching thread

Iron

Stenciling kit (see page 65)

Design templates on page 141

PREPARE TO PRINT

1. Transfer the designs from the templates to the stencil film, as described on page 60. Cut a piece of stencil film for each template. To create the stem for the table runner, draw a ¼" x 10" (6 mm x 25.4 cm) rectangle onto a piece of stencil film and cut out the design.

2. Cut the stencils as described on page 61, leaving a margin around the perimeter of the design to keep the ink from bleeding off of the edge of the stencil onto the fabric.

3. For the table runner, cut one 17" x 90" (43.2 cm x 2.3 m) rectangle of fabric or measure your table and adjust the length or width of your table runner accordingly. Cut four 18" (45.7 cm) squares of fabric for the napkins and use the leftover fabric for test printing.

4. Mix your custom colors as described on page 14; make sure to shake the jars of textile paint well before using and mix your paint thoroughly after every addition of black you make. The yellow for the flower petals was used directly from the jar and did not require any custom mixing. Here are the formulas for the two shades of gray:

For the light gray flower centers, use two spoonfuls of white ink and slowly add half a spoonful of black ink, then a dab of yellow, until you have a desired shade of warm gray.

For the dark gray leaves and stem on the table runner, use two spoonfuls of white ink and slowly add black ink until you reach the desired shade.

5. Make a test print as described on page 62.

A. Center the stem stencil

B. Print leaves and stem

C. Use fresh dauber for each color

ADD THE PATTERN AND FINISH

6. In preparation for printing, iron the cut fabric pieces to eliminate any wrinkles or creases.

7. Take the piece of fabric you cut for the table runner and fold in half widthwise, then finger-press a crease to mark the middle. Open it flat. Peel away the paper backing of the stem stencil and place it on the table runner so the centerline of the design is equidistant from the edges of the fabric and the middle of the design is on the fold line. **(A)**

8. Smooth out any wrinkles with your fingers, making sure that the stencil makes full contact with the fabric.

9. Refer to the stencil printing instructions on page 62 as needed: Print the leaves and stem first using the dark gray paint. Add thin even layers and let dry slightly. **(B)**

10. To add the floral design, begin stippling the light gray paint into the center. Since this two-color design uses only one stencil, it is very important that you confine the light gray to the center of the stencil only.

11. When you are satisfied with the coverage of the light gray paint, let it dry a bit before beginning to print the petals. Repeat the printing process with the yellow paint, using a fresh dauber. **(C)**

12. To print the napkins, begin in the bottom right-hand corner, leaving a margin of about 1½" (3.8 cm) between the cut areas of the stencil and the edge of the fabric. Print in a similar fashion as in steps 10 and 11, printing the centers with warm gray and then adding the yellow petals.

13. Allow all of the ink to dry completely and then slowly peel away the stencil film, being careful that it does not rip or tear. Repeat the printing process for the other three napkins.

14. Make a narrow machine hem to finish the raw edges of each napkin and the table runner. Heat-set the textile paint according to the manufacturer's instructions.

> **HINT:** It is very easy to adapt this design for a different-sized table runner. Since you cut the stem yourself, you can make it to suit your custom dimensions; you could also add multiple repeats of the pattern used in this project.

FOLK ART BARN LAMP

THE DESIGN FOR THIS STENCILED BARN LAMP WAS INSPIRED BY SCAN-DINAVIAN FOLK ART—AND MY DREAM OF HAVING A COUNTRY KITCHEN IN A LITTLE HOUSE IN THE WOODS. THE CLEAN LINES OF THE INDUS-TRIAL PENDANT LAMP AND THE GEOMETRIC FLORAL PATTERN PLAY WELL TOGETHER, GIVING THE TRADITIONAL MOTIFS A MODERN SPIN.

STENCIL MATERIAL   Adhesive stencil film

SURFACE & SUPPLIES

White pendant lamp, 10" (25.4 cm) in diameter (I purchased mine at IKEA)

All-surface acrylic paint in the color of your choice (I used Martha Stewart Multi-Surface Satin Acrylic Craft Paint in Wild Blueberry)

½" (1.3 cm) foam dauber

¼" (6 mm) paintbrush

Single-hole punch

Stenciling kit (see page 65)

Design template on page 135

PREPARE TO PRINT

1. Remove the lamp from its packaging and set aside the cord and any installation materials. Use a damp cloth to wipe away any dirt or dust from the surface and let dry completely.

2. Transfer the design from the template to the stencil film as described on page 60.

3. Cut the stencils as detailed on page 61. Create a separate stencil for the flower with the single-hole punch, using the template as a guide to punch out the petals. Leave at least ¾" (1.9 cm) margin around the petals to prevent the paint from bleeding over the edge. **(A)**

A. Create flower and stem stencils

B. Secure the stencil

C. Print the stem

D. Peel away stencil slowly

E. Print the petals

F. Invert the design and repeat

ADD THE PATTERN AND FINISH

4. Peel away the paper backing from the stencil film. Gently place the leaf-and-stem stencil sticky-side down on your lamp, having the stem start about ¾" (1.9 cm) from the lamp's edge; press in place with your fingers. **(B)** Use your fingertips to gently work out any air bubbles and make sure that the stencil is adhered securely to the surface of your lamp.

5. Print the first design (see page 62), being sure to deliver a light, even coat of paint. **(C)** Let the paint dry for a few minutes—acrylic paint is fast-drying—before gently peeling away the stencil. **(D)** If you have any unwanted bits of paint on the lamp, use a damp cotton swab to wipe them away.

6. Place the circular petal stencil so the dots are approximately ¼" (6 mm) from the top of the stem, gently pressing the stencil to the surface of the lamp. Repeat the printing process as in step 5. **(E)** Allow to dry and carefully pull the stencil away.

7. To create the pattern repeat, invert the design and print the petals first. Allow approximately 1¼" (3.2 cm) between the leaves for each subsequent print. **(F)** The image should repeat 12 times around the perimeter of a lamp this size. Use a small paintbrush to fill in any imperfections in the design if needed. Let the paint dry completely. Hang the lamp according to the manufacturer's instructions.

MODERN SIDE CHAIR

I FOUND THIS MID-CENTURY MODERN CHAIR AND WAS SMITTEN WITH ITS CLEAN LINES AND INTERESTING SHAPE. I RE-COVERED THE SEAT WITH A GRAPHIC HAND-STENCILED COTTON COVER AND USED A REVERSE STENCIL TECHNIQUE TO EMBELLISH THE BACK WITH A SIMPLE LEAF DESIGN.

STENCIL MATERIAL Contact paper (chair back); Stencil film blank (chair seat)

SURFACE & SUPPLIES (CHAIR BACK)

Chair with a removable cushion

Sandpaper (optional)

Latex primer in white

Latex paint in cream or antique white

4" (10.2 cm) foam paint roller

Small paint tray

Painter's tape

Stenciling kit (see page 65)

Design template on page 135

NOTE: For the reverse stencil on the chair back, I used opaque contact paper instead of repositionable stencil film. Because contact paper is thicker and has more tack, it adhered to the wood better and stayed put through several coats of paint. The opaque color also made it easier to see on the dark wooden chair, and if necessary I could reposition the contact paper several times to get the placement just right.

SURFACE & SUPPLIES (CHAIR SEAT)

1¼ yards (1.1 m) medium-weight unbleached cotton or linen, at least 44" (1.1 m) wide, pre-washed (see Note)

¾ yard (68.6 cm) gray felt, at least 44" (1.1 m) wide

All-surface acrylic paint in 2 colors of your choice (I used Martha Stewart Multi-Surface Satin Acrylic Craft Paint in Yellow Jacket and Gray Wolf)

½" (1.3 cm) stencil brush or foam dauber

Repositionable adhesive spray

Staple gun and staples

Stenciling kit (see page 65)

Design template on page 136

NOTE: You may need to adjust the amount of cotton or linen yardage recommended for the chair seat based on the size of your seat cushion. You will need to allow at least 6" (15.2 cm) on all sides for tacking underneath the seat, so measure as necessary. It is possible you will need to purchase more felt as well.

A. Adjust stencil placement and attach

B. Apply primer over stencils

C. Peel away stencil carefully

PREPARE TO PRINT (CHAIR BACK)

1. Remove the seat cushion from the chair and clean the seat back. If you are using a vintage chair, sand any dings in the wood so the surface is smooth. Photocopy the design template and transfer it onto the paper backing of the contact paper using the technique outlined on page 60.

2. Cut the stencil using the technique outlined on page 61, but use the cut-out design as the template.

3. Use a small piece of artist tape to gently tape your stencils onto the back of your chair to help you decide where to place them. **(A)** When you are satisfied, peel away the paper backing from the contact paper and apply the stencils to the back of your chair, folding over any edges that might be extending beyond the frame. Press in place securely, using your fingertips to work out any air bubbles.

4. Tape off any parts of the chair that need protection from unwanted paint. If you need to protect the floor in your workspace, place your chair on a drop cloth.

5. Use the foam roller to paint a layer of primer over the back of your chair, also painting over the stencils. **(B)** Wash and dry your foam roller and paint tray while allowing the primer to dry completely.

ADD THE PATTERN (CHAIR BACK)

6. Spoon a line of latex paint into the paint tray and push the roller through the paint to coat evenly. Roll a layer of paint over the stencils onto the back of your chair. Allow the paint to dry and add a second coat. When the paint is dry to the touch, peel off the stencils carefully. **(C)**

PREPARE TO PRINT (CHAIR SEAT)

7. While you are letting the first coat of paint dry on the chair back, you can print the fabric for the seat cushion. Begin by ironing the prewashed fabric so it is crisp and free of wrinkles.

8. Transfer the template onto the stencil film blank as described on page 60 and cut the stencil as outlined on page 61. Do not be concerned if each square is a tiny bit irregular, because these slight variations will make your final pattern more interesting and unique.

9. Spray the back of the stencil with a thin coat of repositionable adhesive spray. Position the stencil in the upper left-hand corner of your fabric, pressing it flat.

10. Shake the jars of paint well. Make a custom mix (see page 14): Use 4 spoonfuls of yellow paint and add a dab of gray; stir thoroughly. Add more gray as necessary until you reach your desired shade.

11. Make a test print on a small piece of fabric, following the instructions on page 62 as needed, and allow to dry completely. Remember that paint will usually dry a bit darker on your fabric, so let it dry completely to make sure you are satisfied with the color before printing on your final project.

ADD THE PATTERN (CHAIR SEAT)

12. Start printing in the upper left-hand corner of the fabric, moving from left to right; refer to the instructions on page 62 as needed. Place your stencil so there is approximately ½" (1.3 cm) between each repeat. **(D)** If the stencil begins to lose tack, spray another light coat of adhesive on the back and continue printing until the entire piece of fabric is covered.

13. Lay flat or hang to dry.

D. Print seat cover

E. Add felt backing

F. Reattach cushion

COMPLETE THE PROJECT

14. Place the seat fabric pattern-side down on a clean work surface.

15. Place the seat cushion top-side down in the center of your fabric and pull the fabric up and over the front center of the seat cushion; be sure it is very taut. Staple the fabric to the cushion.

16. Repeat step 15 at the center of each side of the cushion, again pulling the fabric very taut each time. Then pull and staple the fabric around the entire perimeter of the cushion. Trim the fabric, leaving about 2" (5.1 cm) of excess.

17. Place the seat cushion on top of the felt and trace around it with a pen or pencil. Cut about 1" (2.5 cm) inside the marked line and then staple the felt to the bottom of the cushion, covering the raw edges of the printed fabric for a clean finish. **(E)**

18. Reattach the cushion to the chair, cutting through the felt with a utility knife to expose the holes for the screws as necessary. **(F)**

HINT: The techniques used in this project could also be used to dress up a plain new chair or applied to a different piece of furniture for a fun modern accent.

SILK INFINITY SCARF

THIS PROJECT COMES TOGETHER QUICKLY AND EASILY BECAUSE IT BE-
GINS WITH A STORE-BOUGHT SILK SCARF. THE LINE MOTIF I CHOSE TO
PRINT ON IT COMPLEMENTS MANY GARMENTS, AND THE RICH SALMON
COLOR IS FLATTERING TO ALMOST ALL SKIN TONES. BUT, OF COURSE,
YOU CAN CUSTOMIZE TO YOUR TASTE BY CHANGING THE STENCIL AND/
OR THE COLOR.

STENCIL MATERIAL   Stencil film blank

SURFACE & SUPPLIES

White silk scarf with rolled hem, 15" x 60" (38.1 x 152.4 cm) (I used a Jacquard scarf blank;
see Resources, page 142)

Dye attractrant pen (I used a Jacquard Color Magnet pen)

Textile paint in the color of your choice (I used Jacquard Dye-Na-Flow in Salmon)

Large glass bowl or bucket (see Note below)

Hair dryer (optional)

Needle and matching thread

Iron

Soft rag

Stenciling kit (see page 65)

Design template on page 137

NOTE: Although these dyes are nontoxic and water-based, I suggest using a dedicated
container for dyeing that will not be used for food again.

PREPARE TO PRINT

1. Transfer the stencil design onto the stencil blank and cut the stencil using a sharp utility blade as described on page 61.

2. Set your iron to the Silk setting and gently press to remove any wrinkles or creases. Spread out the scarf on your work surface and smooth. Place the stencil so the design runs horizontally along the length of the scarf, as shown in the photo. **(A)**

A. Arrange the stencil

B. Apply dye attractant to stencil

C. Cover with pattern from left to right

ADD THE PATTERN

3. The textile paint used in this project will leave a subtle glow of color on the body of the scarf, but the areas where the dye attractant is applied will be rich and vibrant. Shake the dye attractant pen well and gently squeeze until the sponge applicator is saturated. Hold the stencil in place with your hands and use the applicator to dab the attractant through the stencil, working from left to right across the scarf. **(B)** The dye attractant is a pale yellow color, so look closely to make sure you have not missed large spots inside the stencil as you were working.

4. Turn the stencil upside down and wipe away any dye attractant that has spilled on the underside of the stencil with a rag or paper towel. Leave the stencil upside down and continue using the dye attractant pen to add pattern to the scarf, going all way to the edges and overlapping the patterns slightly as you work for a more organic look. **(C)** Cover the entire scarf with pattern, flipping the stencil as you work.

5. You must make sure that the scarf is completely dry before moving on to the dyeing step. Use a hair dryer for quick results or let it dry overnight.

6. In a large bowl or bucket, add the entire jar of textile paint and 1 cup (236 ml) water; stir well. Place the silk scarf into the color bath and stir until it is completely saturated. Let the scarf soak for at least 20 minutes, stirring occasionally.

7. Remove the scarf from the bucket and rinse in warm water until the water runs clear.

COMPLETE THE PROJECT

8. Allow the scarf to dry completely and then follow the manufacturer's instructions to make the color permanent.

9. Use the needle with matching thread to stitch the short ends of the scarf together so it forms a loop.

PLAYFUL
CERAMIC PLATTERS

SOMETIMES INSPIRATION COMES FROM UNEXPECTED PLACES. I FOUND A SET OF DRAFTING STENCILS AT THE ART STORE AND USED THE SIMPLE GRAPHIC SHAPES TO DRESS UP THESE PLAIN WHITE PLATTERS. AN OPAQUE MARKER MADE ESPECIALLY FOR USE ON CERAMICS AND GLASS MAKES THE PROCESS SIMPLE AND THE RESULTS CHIC. YOU CAN MODIFY THE NUMBER OF DESIGNS TO FIT ALMOST ANY PLATE OR PLATTER.

STENCIL MATERIALS   1 flow chart-type stencil; 1 architectural-type stencil

SURFACE & SUPPLIES

2 white ceramic platters with flat, shallow bottoms, 1 small and 1 large: these are 11" x 6" (27.9 cm x 15.2 cm) and 14" x 8" (35.6 cm x 20.3 cm)

2 enamel paint markers in the color of your choice (I used TransformMason Enamel Markers in Black)

Ceramic plate for test printing

Cotton balls

Rubbing alcohol

Acetone fingernail polish remover

Stenciling kit (see page 65)

NOTE: This project is designed to allow you to use purchased stencils as a medium but add your own personal spin to the project. Feel free to experiment and use similar shapes from any ready-made stencil to create your own designs, using these instructions as a guide; office supply stores stock all kinds of interesting stencils, too. Depending on the sizes and shapes of your platters, cut individual templates free from the stencils so they will lie flat against the platters.

PREPARE TO PRINT

1. Wash the platters in hot soapy water and dry thoroughly. Wipe down the printable surface of the platters with a cotton ball soaked in rubbing alcohol to remove any remaining surface dirt or oil.

2. Test the enamel marker on scrap paper by depressing the tip of the marker until you have an even, opaque flow of ink.

3. Make a test print as described on page 62. Fill in a shape from one of the stencils, first starting the flow of ink as in step 2, refreshing it as needed. If you make a mistake, use a cotton ball or swab soaked in nail polish remover to remove the ink while it is still wet.

A. Hold stencil in place and fill in shape

B. Invert each motif

C. Apply pattern to edges of large platter

ADD THE PATTERN (SMALL PLATTER)

4. To decorate the smaller platter, use a large circle from an architectural-type stencil. (I started with a 1¼" [3.2 cm] circle.) Starting 1" or 2" (2.5 to 5.1 cm) from the lip of the platter, fill in the circle with smooth, even strokes, holding the stencil against the platter with your hands. **(A)** If there are light spots, allow the ink to dry and gently cover over them after shaking the pen and refreshing the flow of ink.

5. Use the straight edge of the stencil to draw a line from the center of the circle so your design looks like a lollipop. Allow to dry.

6. Find an appropriately sized triangle on the architectural stencil and fill it in as shown, placing it about halfway down the center of the line you drew in step 5. Turn the drafting stencil over and fill in another triangle on the opposite side of the line. Repeat this process to decorate the platter, inverting every other design, until you have covered the base of the platter. **(B)**

ADD THE PATTERN (LARGE PLATTER)

7. To decorate the larger platter, use a group of triangles from the flow chart-type stencil. (Feel free to substitute similar shapes if your stencil has motifs you find intriguing. If your stencil does not have the same configuration of triangles that mine had, it is easy to replicate the feel of this pattern with any group of small, repeated images.) Place the stencil in one corner of the platter and fill in each of the triangles with the enamel ink marker, holding the stencil in place with your fingers. Slide the stencil to the left approximately ¼" (6 mm) or so, depending on your pattern, and repeat. **(C)**

8. Continue printing the small pattern around the entire perimeter of your platter. Remember that you can touch up any imperfections before the ink dries by using a cotton swab dipped in nail polish remover.

COMPLETE THE PROJECT

9. Allow your platters to dry for at least 1 hour, and then follow the instructions given by the marker's manufacturer to heat-set them in the oven. The enamel ink you used on them is non-toxic and food safe; enjoy them often! To care for the platters, simply hand wash and dry.

STRIPED
STORAGE BASKET

BASKETS ARE A BEAUTIFUL AND PRACTICAL WAY TO ADD STORAGE TO YOUR HOME. I DREW INSPIRATION FOR THESE FROM THE TRADITIONAL HANDWOVEN BASKETS OF MEXICO. THE COLORFUL STENCILED STRIPES WILL QUICKLY BRIGHTEN ANY ROOM.

STENCIL MATERIALS   Artist tape, 1" (2.5 cm) wide

SURFACE & SUPPLIES

Large wicker basket, approximately 23" (58.4 cm) wide x 18" (45.7 cm) deep x 18" (45.7 cm) high

4 stencil brushes, 2 brushes each 1" (2.5 cm) and 2 brushes each ½" (1.3 cm) wide

All-surface acrylic paint in 4 colors of your choice (I used Martha Stewart Multi-Surface Satin Acrylic Craft Paint in Party Streamer, Geranium, Chipotle, and Granny Smith)

Clear acrylic sealer

Stenciling kit (see page 65)

NOTE: If your basket is significantly different in size than the one used in this project, you may need to adjust the pattern to fit.

PREPARE TO PRINT

1. Place a fabric or plastic drop cloth on your work surface to protect it from paint; if your basket is very large you may want to work on the floor instead of a table.

2. Measure 2½" (6.4 cm) from the bottom of the basket and run a band of tape around the entire perimeter of the basket. Measure 3" (7.6 cm) from the top edge of the first band of tape, and add another band around the entire basket. I suggest you measure every few inches (centimeters) as you add subsequent bands of tape to make sure that your stripes are not crooked.

3. Measure 2" (5.1 cm) from the top of the second band of tape, and add a third band. Measure 1¼" (3.2 cm) from the top of the third band of tape, and add a fourth band of artist tape. Use your fingertips to make sure the tape is well adhered to the basket and there are no lumps, air bubbles, or other disturbances that might cause paint to leak under your taped lines. **(A)**

A. Layout design

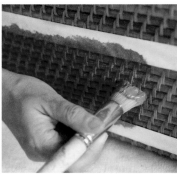

B. Stipple paint into marked areas

C. Add green stripes with small stencil brush

ADD THE PATTERN

4. Squeeze a silver-dollar-sized amount of the fuchsia paint onto your palette and use one of the 1" (2.5 cm) stencil brushes to pick up a small amount of paint. Tap on your palette to distribute the paint evenly. Refer to page 62 for instructions on how to load and stipple, if needed.

5. Paint the 3" (7.6 cm) stripe on the basket. Use the bristles of the brush to get down inside the wicker so you are not just coating the exterior of the basket in paint; the basket will have better coverage and a more "woven" look if you follow this instruction. Add more paint to your palette as needed. **(B)**

6. While the fuchsia paint is drying, move on to the 2" (5.1 cm) stripe and paint that stripe orange, but do not remove any of the tape.

7. Refill the fuchsia and orange paint on your palette if needed and use the ½" (1.3 cm) stencil brushes to paint the 1" (2.5 cm) stripe, using a separate brush for each color. Paint alternating dabs of fuchsia and orange around the entire basket, making each dab approximately 2" (5.1 cm) long.

8. Wash the ½" (1.3 cm) stencil brushes and let dry. Set one of these brushes aside to use with the green paint.

9. Allow the paint to dry, carefully peel away the tape, and discard.

10. Run a line of tape over the bottom edge of the fuchsia stripe and add another band of tape 1" (2.5 cm) below it. Fill that stripe in with the dark red color.

11. Allow to dry and peel away and discard the tape. Use the fine-tipped brush from your stenciling kit to fill in any gaps or imperfect spots in your stripes.

12. Now use the tape and create small ½" x 3" (1.3 x 7.6 cm) stripes along the basket; fill them in with bright green paint, using the small stencil brush. **(C)**

COMPLETE THE PROJECT

13. Remove all tape from the basket. Allow the paint to dry for several hours (or overnight) and then spray the basket with a light coat of protective sealant, working outside or in a well-ventilated area.

> **HINT:** I suggest using a free and easy approach when adding the bright green stripes. I added them every 8" to 14" (20.3 to 35.6 cm) along the edges of the fuchsia and orange stripes, both above and below.

STARBURST WALL PRINTS

THIS SIMPLE ALLOVER PATTERN ADDS A HUGE DOSE OF PERSONALITY TO
ANY SPACE. I CHOSE TO PRINT MY STARBURSTS IN A DARK CHOCOLATE
BROWN FOR A BOLD, SOPHISTICATED RESULT, BUT YOU COULD EASILY
CHANGE THE COLOR SCHEME TO SUIT YOUR TASTE.

STENCIL MATERIAL   Stencil film blank

SURFACE & SUPPLIES

All-surface acrylic paint in the color of your choice (I used 2 jars of Martha Stewart Multi-Surface
Satin Acrylic Craft Paint in Vanilla Bean)

¾" (1.9 cm) foam dauber (one or more depending on how large a space you are covering)

Repositionable adhesive spray

Drop cloth

Stenciling kit (see page 65)

Design template on page 139

NOTE: If you are filling an entire wall with pattern, consider this a weekend project. Two small
2-oz (59 ml) containers of inexpensive all-surface acrylic paint is a generous amount for an 8' x
8' (2.4 x 2.4 m) wall. You will also need extra daubers, perhaps three or four. If you plan to paint
your base wall before adding the pattern, use standard latex paint in an eggshell or satin finish;
purchase enough for two coats.

PREPARE TO PRINT

1. If you are not painting your walls, wash them well with a soft rag and gentle all-purpose clean-
er and allow to dry before you begin stenciling. If you want to paint the walls a different base
color, follow standard procedures to prime and paint.

2. If necessary, place a drop cloth on the floor to catch any spills, unless you used one to paint
your walls and it is still in place.

3. Use the tools in your stenciling kit and the techniques outlined on page 60 to transfer the design to your stencil film and make the stencil.

A. Rotate stencil between each printing

B. Repeat to cover entire wall

C. Touch up with small paint-brush if needed

ADD THE PATTERN

4. Spray the back of the stencil with repositionable adhesive spray. Place the stencil on the upper left-hand corner of the wall and press in place so it lies flat, paying close attention to the center points of the design. This is where it is most likely to lift away from the wall.

5. Load a small amount of paint onto your dauber and stipple a thin layer of paint through the stencil until it is opaque. Allow to dry slightly and then apply a second coat if necessary. After the paint is dry, peel the stencil from the wall and wipe away any excess paint.

6. Place the stencil 6" to 8" (15.2 to 20.3 cm) from the first print, repeating steps 4 and 5 as you move across the entire wall (or walls). After every few prints, take a few steps back from the wall and examine your work to see if you need to tweak the pattern. I suggest a freeform approach instead of printing this stencil in orderly rows. Try changing the orientation of the stencil by 45° for each new print. **(A)**

COMPLETE THE PROJECT

7. Apply more adhesive spray to the stencil as needed so it makes firm contact with the wall. When you reach the floor, ceiling, or edge of the wall, turn the stencil so you get it as close to the edge as possible. Continue printing until you have covered the desired area on the wall (or walls) with pattern. **(B)**

8. If needed, use the small paintbrush to touch up the edges of the stencil prints. **(C)**

PAINT

PAINTING BASICS

THE FOCUS OF THIS CHAPTER IS CREATING PATTERNS BY HAND. UNLIKE IN THE PREVIOUS CHAPTERS, YOU WILL NOT BE USING RESISTS LIKE STENCILS OR TOOLS LIKE STAMPS TO CREATE THE DESIGNS. FOR THE PROJECTS HERE, YOU RELY ON YOUR OWN HANDS AND EYES AND MY SIMPLE-TO-FOLLOW INSTRUCTIONS.

If you are at all hesitant about painting patterns by hand, I hope that this chapter will erase your anxiety and replace it with the excitement of possibility. I am giving you permission to embellish your life now, so all you need to do is jump in and get started! If you are already confident about drawing, painting, and making patterns, then the activities presented in the next few pages may serve as jumping-off points for creating your own designs. I hope the projects will as well.

KEEP A SKETCHBOOK

An essential part of creating successful freehand patterns is getting comfortable drawing and making marks. A sketchbook will be an indispensable tool as you move through this chapter; use it to practice making patterns and capture inspiration as it comes to you. Many people stop expressing themselves visually as children and then progressively stiffen, gripped by the fear that if it does not look perfect there is no point to making it at all. This could not be further from the truth! Anyone can create a lovely painted pattern, no matter their skill level or artistic experience.

You can practice your designs anywhere—at home, at the doctor's office, on the subway. When you have a few free minutes, get into the habit of picking up a pen, pencil, or brush, and making a few marks in your sketchbook. Once you have a collection of these informal drawings, look them over and see what patterns you are attracted to. Are they geometric shapes such as circles, lines, or squares? Or elements from nature like leaves, clouds, or branches? Do your doodles have clean lines or are they more irregular and expressive? Look at these drawings and notice how they make patterns. Try combining them to create new possibilities for your own freehand pattern designs, or imagine turning them into custom stencils or hand-carved stamps for a project later on.

ACTIVITIES FOR INSPIRATION

Unlike the Stamp and Stencil chapters, there are no specific techniques that you need to learn for the projects in the Paint section. They are all executed simply, primarily with a brush and paint, and the most important "tool" you need is your own imagination. Here are some suggestions to make the process easier for you, especially if you are new to freehand painting. Try each of these four activities and work directly in your sketchbook or record your results there.

1. THINK SIMPLE

The most appealing freehand patterns are often the most basic. Geometric designs such as stripes, polka dots, and grids are classic elements and deliver consistent, stylish results. The patterns in the Paint chapter are kept intentionally simple and easy, with no special skills required.

Activity: Draw a collection of geometric designs, either combining them on a single page or devoting an entire page to each type.

PAINTING TOOLS AND MATERIALS:

1. Brayer and all-surface acrylic paint 2. Acrylic artist palette
3. Flower-shaped plastic palette 4. Paintbrushes 5. Textile
paint 6. Canvas drop cloth 7. Paint swatches: top, linen;
center, canvas; bottom, silk

2. EMBRACE IRREGULARITY

A bit of irregularity should be embraced when working on painted patterns—it adds personality and charm to your designs. In my opinion, many patterns are greatly improved by seeing the mark of the artist, and what could be viewed as an imperfection or "mistake" is often what gives your design soul and visual interest.

Activity: Decide on a simple design and quickly use it to make a page full of pattern. Do not fuss over making the designs perfect, just sketch. When you are done, look at the page and see how the imperfections give your patternmaking personality.

3. SEE PATTERN EVERYWHERE

Another way to practice and grow more comfortable with freehand patternmaking is to design with three-dimensional objects, such as stones, leaves, cut paper, matchsticks, or coins. When you create a pattern that you love, snap a picture of it or draw the pattern in your sketchbook. Document your process so you can remember your designs to recreate them later, or use them as the foundation for another pattern.

Activity: Take your objects and arrange them on a flat surface, such as a table or the floor. What kind of patterns can you create out of a pile of wooden matches? How do they look when they are arranged in lines, stacked, crossed, or tossed? Try lining up stones or coins into stripes, or scatter them for an all-over dot pattern; this exercise was the inspiration for the Solar Print Scarf on page 126. To create more complex patterns, consider bringing two kinds of objects together.

4. TEST YOUR TOOLS

Before you begin working on a project, take a bit of time to get comfortable with your tools and materials. Explore how a felt-tipped pen glides along a piece of ceramic, or feel how your brush dipped in paint moves differently across a piece of cotton than it does over rough canvas. Each time you explore the way your materials look and feel, you gain valuable information that will make your final patterns more appealing, expressive, and successful.

Activity: Gather up at least three different types of fabric and use the same brush and pigment on each one. Explore how the texture and thickness of the fabric affects the final result.

The fabric on which you work can have a big impact on the final result. Notice how different the pigment looks on these materials: top, canvas; center, silk; and bottom, linen.

READY, SET, ...

Start with the project that most excites you! The tools and pigment that you will use in the projects have been discussed in Getting Started (page 13), so refer back to that material as needed. All the supplies you need will be provided in the project instructions. Of course, you will need to prepare your workspace and follow the same kind of cleanup practices as in the previous chapters.

You can start small, by drawing on a ceramic salt cellar (Anemone Salt Cellar, page 115) or by painting a stylish canvas-and-leather clutch (Painterly Party Clutch, page 118). Or dive in right away and work big on the hand-painted duvet and pillowcase set (Windswept Bedding Set, page 130). Find what inspires you and begin to add more pattern to your home and wardrobe with freehand painting.

BRUSHSTROKE KITCHEN LINENS

THESE THIRSTY COTTON TEA TOWELS ARE PRACTICAL AND A GREAT WAY TO ADD PANACHE TO YOUR KITCHEN—THE SIMPLE BRUSHSTROKE PATTERNS AND BRIGHT COLORS ARE STYLISH AND MODERN. THIS IS A GREAT FIRST PROJECT FOR PAINTING ON FABRIC. I SUGGEST HAVING A LARGE STACK OF TEA TOWELS CUT, BECAUSE ONCE YOU START PAINTING IT IS HARD TO STOP. THESE MAKE WONDERFUL GIFTS, SO MAKE PLENTY TO GO AROUND.

SURFACE & SUPPLIES

1¾ yards (1.6 m) 100% cotton muslin, at least 44" (1.1 m) wide

Textile paint in 3 colors of your choice (I used Jacquard Textile Color in Sky Blue, Yellow Ochre, and White)

Acrylic artist palette or plastic cups

Plastic spoon

¾" (1.9 cm) flat paintbrush

Canvas drop cloth, newsprint, or kraft paper

Jar of water

Rag or paper towels

Iron

Sewing machine and related supplies, including matching thread

NOTE: The yardage listed will make 4 towels, with extra fabric for test painting. All-cotton flour sack towels are a great alternative to muslin if you do not want to cut and sew your own towels.

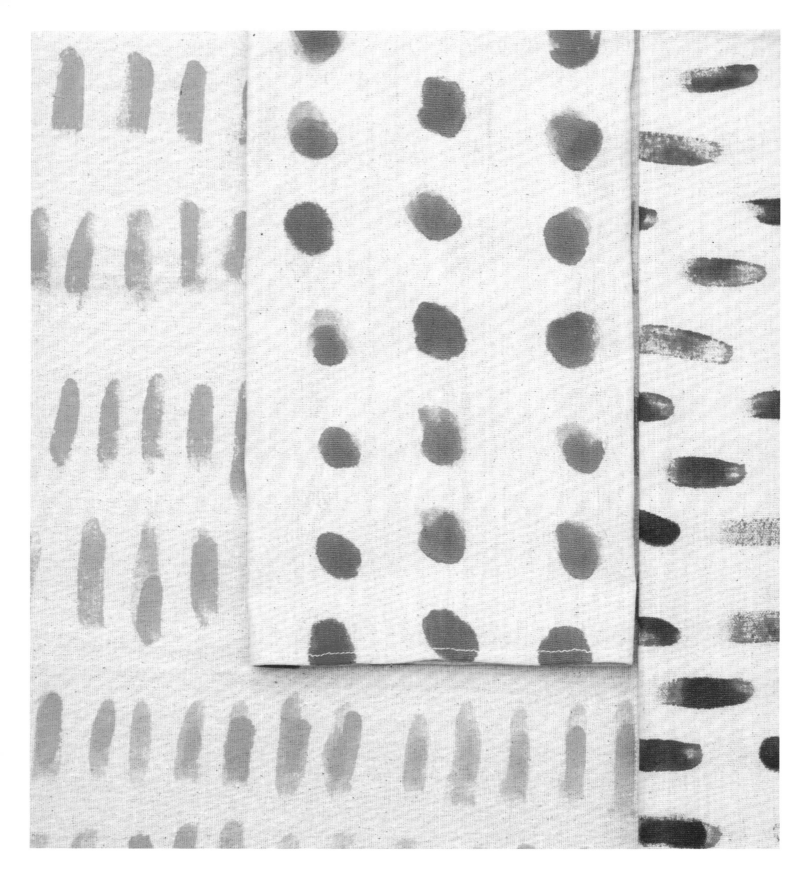

PREPARE TO PAINT

1. Wash, tumble dry, and iron the cotton muslin. Cut the fabric into 4 rectangles each 19" x 26" (48.3 x 66 cm) and set aside. Take the remaining muslin and cut it into swatches for testing your colors and brushstroke patterns.

2. Protect your work surface with a drop cloth or paper and prepare to mix your textile paints. Make custom colors as follows, referring to the complete instructions for mixing colors on page 14 as needed. Mix each shade thoroughly before you begin painting. **(A)**

For the bright blue polka dots, mix 1 tablespoon (14.8 ml) blue, ½ teaspoon (2.5 ml) white, and 1 tablespoon (14.8 ml) water. Mix well and add ½ teaspoon (2.5 ml) more white at a time until the desired shade is reached.

For the dark green brushstrokes, mix 1 tablespoon (14.8 ml) blue, ½ teaspoon (2.5 ml) yellow, and 1 tablespoon (14.8 ml) water to start. Mix well and add ½ teaspoon (2.5 ml) more yellow at a time until the desired shade of green is reached.

For the aqua brushstrokes, mix 1 tablespoon (14.8 ml) blue, 1 tablespoon (14.8 ml) white, ½ teaspoon (2.5 ml) yellow, and 1 tablespoon (14.8 ml) water.

3. Test the colors and get a feel for painting on the cotton muslin. When you are satisfied with your colors and have practiced making brushstrokes, move on to the tea towels.

A. Mix custom colors

B. Paint pattern

C. Heat-set the paint

ADD THE PATTERN AND FINISH

4. Place one of the cotton muslin rectangles on your work surface and smooth away any wrinkles or creases. Choose a color and begin painting on the unfinished tea towel, using the patterns in the photo at left as a guide. Paint each of the tea towels, washing and drying your brush each time you change colors (or use a separate brush for each color). Let the towels dry completely. **(B)**

5. Follow the manufacturer's instructions to heat-set the textile paint, making it permanent. **(C)**

6. Make a narrow machine hem to finish the raw edges of each tea towel.

CORAL DOTS
DESSERT PLATES

THIS SIMPLE FREEHAND DOT PATTERN DRESSES UP PLAIN DISHES. I CHOSE A BRIGHT CORAL ORANGE PAINT FOR MY PATTERN AND USED IT ON PLATES WITH A GOLD RIM FOR A METALLIC ACCENT. YOU CAN CREATE THIS PATTERN ON A SET OF DISHES THAT YOU ALREADY HAVE IN YOUR CUPBOARD OR USE THE PATTERN TO TIE TOGETHER THRIFTED DISHES INTO A MATCHING SET.

SURFACE & SUPPLIES

4 white dessert plates, approximately 8½" (21.6 cm) in diameter

Ceramic or all-surface acrylic paint in the color of your choice (I used Martha Stewart Multi-Surface Satin Acrylic Craft Paint in Geranium)

¼" (6 mm) foam dauber

Ceramic plate for test painting

¼" (6 mm) or smaller fine-tipped paintbrush

Acrylic artist palette

Rubbing alcohol

Cotton balls

Cotton swabs

PREPARE TO PAINT

1. Wash your plates in hot, soapy water and dry completely. Take a cotton ball soaked in rubbing alcohol and wipe down the entire surface of each plate to remove any remaining dirt or oil.

2. Squeeze out a bit of ink about the size of a quarter onto the artist palette and pick up a small amount of paint with the tip of your foam dauber. Gently tap the end of the dauber on your test plate to evenly distribute the paint.

3. Pick up more paint as needed and begin testing the pattern on the plate. Come down onto the surface of the plate flat with the dauber sponge and press gently, lifting straight up when you are done. The dauber should leave an opaque circle of paint. If it is too light add a bit more paint, but if the paint is pooling around the edges dab away some of the paint and try again until the results of the dauber prints are consistent. **(A)**

A. Practice the pattern

B. Fill plate with dots

C. Refine the design

ADD THE PATTERN AND FINISH

4. Fill your dauber with paint and blot as in step 2. Starting at the rim of one of the plates, begin painting dots in a U shape around the edge of the plate. Use the sponge tip of the dauber to come down flat on the surface of the plate as you practiced in step 3, painting polka-dot scallops around the edge of the plate. Aim for about 10 scallops on an 8½" (21.6 cm) plate, each approximately 1½" to 2" (3.8 to 5.1 cm) wide and 2" (5.1 cm) tall. Refill the dauber with paint, blot, and repeat to continue adding pattern. **(B)** Embrace irregularity!

5. After you have finished with one plate, set it aside to dry and continue adding the polka-dot scallops to the rest of your dishes. If there are dots that you are not happy with, use a moist cotton swab to remove them while the paint is wet. Allow the plate to dry and then continue the pattern.

6. If needed, use the fine-tipped paintbrush to fill in any blank areas or holes in the design. **(C)**

7. Follow the manufacturer's instructions to heat-set or cure the paint. To preserve the decoration, always wash the plates by hand and avoid abrasive scrubbers.

BRAYER PRINT WALL ART

THE RANDOM SHAPES AND PATTERNS THAT RESULT WHEN YOU ROLL AN
INKY BRAYER ONTO PAPER INSPIRED THESE ABSTRACT, GRAPHIC PRINTS.
THIS IS A GREAT WAY TO MAKE ART WITH CHILDREN, OR TO MAKE USE OF
EXTRA INK FROM ANOTHER PROJECT.

SURFACE & SUPPLIES

3 sheets white rag paper for printmaking, each 24" x 36" (61 x 91.4 cm) (I used Rives BFK)

Ink or paint in the color of your choice

1½" (3.8 cm) brayer

Acrylic artist palette

Newsprint

Canvas drop cloth (or additional newsprint)

NOTE: I suggest using a fine printmaking paper for this project. Beautiful paper is not a big
expense and you never know when you might just make a masterpiece!

PREPARE TO PAINT

1. Cover your work surface with a drop cloth or newsprint.

2. Squeeze a quarter-sized amount of ink or paint onto the artist palette. Touch the brayer into the pigment and pick up a small amount on the underside; roll it back and forth on the surface of the palette. Pick up the brayer after each roll, ensuring that the pigment is evenly distributed over the surface of the brayer instead of being pushed across the surface of the artist palette. **(A)**

3. When you have distributed an even layer of ink on your brayer, make a test print on the newsprint. Get a feel for rolling the brayer across paper and experiment with the lines and shapes that you can make. **(B)**

A. Distribute pigment on brayer surface

B. Make a test print

C. Apply freeform pattern

ADD THE PATTERN AND FINISH

4. Clear your work area of any stray pigment and place a piece of rag paper flat on your work surface. Coat the brayer with ink as in step 2 and begin rolling it over the surface of your paper in large, abstract lines. For this pattern there are no rules, so have fun! When you are satisfied with your pattern, move on to the next piece of paper. **(C)**

5. Thoroughly wash and dry your brayer and artist palette between each color and continue to print as desired on the next sheet (or sheets) of paper.

6. Allow the ink or paint to dry thoroughly before framing your art or hanging it on the wall.

ANEMONE SALT CELLAR

I LIKE A SALT CELLAR TO BE FUNCTIONAL FOR EVERYDAY USE, BUT ALSO
STYLISH ENOUGH TO TAKE TO THE TABLE WHEN I AM ENTERTAINING. THE
SHAPES FOUND IN TIDAL POOLS INSPIRED THIS PATTERN, AND THE BLUE-
AND-WHITE COLOR PALETTE IS A NOD TO THE OCEAN.

SURFACE & SUPPLIES

White ceramic salt cellar, approximately 3" (7.6 cm) wide x 2½" (6.4 cm) tall (see Resources, page 142)

Enamel paint marker in the color of your choice (I used a Pebeo Porcelaine 150 Paint Marker in Lapis Blue)

Sketchbook and pen or pencil

Ceramic plate for test printing

Cotton balls

Rubbing alcohol

Acetone fingernail polish remover

PREPARE TO PAINT

1. In your sketchbook, begin by drawing a circle about the size of a nickel. Then draw a smaller circle about the size of a pencil eraser inside the larger circle, placing it slightly off-center.

2. Connect the circles with small lines that look like spokes. Do not be concerned if your circles are slightly off kilter or if your spokes are not straight—these slight imperfections are charming and add character to your lines, making a more interesting pattern.

3. Continue to draw this design so the outer edges of each large circle are touching slightly and the pattern forms a pleasing organic shape. You can draw as many or as few circles as you like, but in general, odd-number combinations (threes, fives, sevens, and so on) are more pleasing to the eye. Experiment with the scale of the pattern by drawing it bigger or smaller in your sketchbook. When you come back to these drawings later, it may inspire a new project or design. **(A)**

4. Wash your practice plate and project dish in hot, soapy water and make sure they are perfectly clean and dry before you begin. Use a cotton ball soaked in rubbing alcohol to wipe the ceramic pieces; if there is any oil or residue on the surface, it will be difficult to draw on and the paint will not adhere properly.

5. Shake your marker well to mix and distribute the pigment, then depress the end to begin the flow of paint. The markers will feel slippery when you are first drawing with them, so make a few marks on your scrap plate to get a feel for the tool. Then sketch for a minute to loosen up your hands before you begin on the salt cellar.

A. Sketch design

B. Apply pattern

C. Decorate inner rim
if desired

ADD THE PATTERN

6. When you are ready, and the pen feels good in your hand, begin drawing the pattern on your dish. Make the first cluster of pattern about 2" (5.1 cm) wide and 1½" (3.8 cm) tall; it may be easiest to identify an area on the salt cellar that you want to decorate and work from one side of it to the other.

7. Continue to decorate the salt cellar with pattern. **(B)** If you make a mistake or the pattern feels off, you can easily remove it before the marker is dry using a cotton ball dipped in nail polish remover. Begin again when the nail polish remover has completely evaporated.

8. If you would like to add a little bit more visual interest, draw a small area of pattern (about the size of a silver dollar) on the inner rim of the dish. **(C)**

COMPLETE THE PROJECT

9. When you are satisfied with your pattern, let the paint dry completely and heat-set the salt cellar per the manufacturer's instructions. After the dish has cooled completely, it is ready to use.

> **HINT:** This motif could be applied to other functional ceramic pieces for the table if you are inspired to create a set.

PAINTERLY
PARTY CLUTCH

THIS CLUTCH WILL TAKE YOU FROM ERRANDS TO COCKTAILS—COMPLIMENTS GUARANTEED. THE PAINTERLY PATTERN CAN BE REPLICATED IN ANY COLOR YOU DESIRE AND THE SUPPLE LEATHER DETAILS ADD LUXURY AND SOPHISTICATION. THE LEATHER FEELS WONDERFUL AGAINST THE SKIN AND REINFORCES THE BOTTOM OF THE CLUTCH, KEEPING THE HAND-PAINTED AREA FREE FROM DIRT AND STAINS.

SURFACE & SUPPLIES

½ yard (45.7 cm) unwashed natural cotton canvas, at least 44" (1.1 m) wide

Textile paint in the color of your choice (I used Jacquard Dye-Na-Flow in Salmon)

½" (1.3 cm) flat paintbrush with firm bristles

Canvas drop cloth or newsprint

Iron

2 pieces soft leather to match paint color, each 3½" x 12½" (8.9 x 31.8 cm)

⅓ yard (30.5 cm) fabric for the lining, in the color or pattern of your choice

¼" (6 mm) double-sided transparent sewing tape

11" (27.9 cm) brass zipper

Sewing machine and related supplies, including matching thread and a leather needle

PREPARE TO PAINT

1. Cut the canvas into a number of 8½" x 12½" (21.6 x 31.8 cm) rectangles. Cut 2 rectangles each 8½" x 12½" (21.6 x 31.8 cm) from the lining fabric.

2. Cover your work surface to protect it from the textile paint.

A. Paint the canvas with vertical strokes

B. Secure leather to canvas

C. Stitch leather to canvas

ADD THE PATTERN

3. Shake the paint well before using; you will work directly from the paint jar for this project. Saturate just the end of your paintbrush with paint. Position the canvas so a longer side is on top and paint from left to right, using firm up-and-down strokes with your brush to push the ink into the fibers of the canvas. Do not be afraid to really go for it when you are painting! Add more paint as needed to your brush and cover the entire surface of the canvas with vertical brush strokes. **(A)**

4. Continue painting rectangles of canvas until you have two with relatively uniform brush strokes. As the paint dries, it will make the canvas buckle. When the pigment is completely dry, iron to flatten the canvas and heat-set the ink, following the manufacturer's recommendations.

COMPLETE THE PROJECT

5. Run a length of double-sided tape along one long edge on the wrong side of each piece of the leather. Peel away the paper backing from the tape. Place the leather tape-side down onto the canvas and use your fingers to press into place. This double-sided tape will help the leather stay in place when you are sewing. **(B)**

6. With the leather needle in your sewing machine, topstitch the leather onto the canvas. Stitch slowly so the leather does not stretch while you are sewing. Repeat with the second piece of canvas and leather. **(C)**

7. Replace the leather needle with an all-purpose sewing needle and have your cotton lining pieces ready. Put a zipper foot on your machine.

8. To install the zipper, place one lining piece right-side up. Place the zipper on top, aligning the right edge of the zipper tape with the right edge of the lining. Now take one exterior piece and place the canvas edge (not the leather edge) facedown on top of the zipper and lining piece, aligning the edges. At this point the zipper should be sandwiched between the two pieces. **(D)**

9. Stitch the edge of the sandwich, using a ¼" (6 mm) seam allowance. Fold back the layers to reveal the zipper. Finger-press in place or pin together to keep them out of the way while you stitch the remaining side.

10. Repeat step 8 to stitch the other side of the zipper, but place the zipper on the left edge of the lining piece. **(E)** Stitch the edges, again using a ¼" (6 mm) seam allowance.

11. Switch to a standard presser foot on your machine. Unzip the zipper and fold the bag so the right sides of the lining pieces face each other and the right sides of the exterior pieces also face one another, making a long rectangle. Pin the edges, folding the zipper tape toward the lining before sewing. **(F)**

12. Use a ½" (1.3 cm) seam allowance and stitch all the way around the perimeter of the clutch, leaving an opening in the lining for turning. Pull the bag right-side out.

13. Topstitch the opening in the lining and push it inside the bag; if needed, adjust the seam at the zipper until it lies flat.

14. If desired, topstitch ¼" (6 mm) away from the zipper to secure the lining inside the bag.

D. Sandwich zipper between lining and canvas

E. Repeat for opposite side

F. Pin lining and canvas edges

HINT: Most canvas has a protective layer of sizing that may cause the paint to bead up rather than soak into the fabric. Using a brush with stiff bristles will help you to push the ink into the fiber of the canvas, giving it the painterly look you see in the finished clutch.

SIMPLE COTTON QUILT

ALTHOUGH THIS COLORFUL CRIB-SIZED QUILT IS SIMPLE TO PAINT AND SEW IN AN AFTERNOON, IT IS TRULY AN HEIRLOOM THAT ANY CHILD OR PARENT WILL CHERISH.

SURFACE & SUPPLIES

2 yards (1.8 m) shot cotton for the quilt top, at least 44" (1.1 m) wide (I used a pale pink and a light gray in this collection)

Textile paint in 3 colors of your choice (I used a variety of Jacquard Dye-Na-Flow paints)

3 flat paintbrushes, each 1" (2.5 cm) wide

Flower-shaped plastic palette or plastic cups

2 yards (1.8 m) cotton for the quilt back, at least 44" (1.1 m) wide

1 package crib-sized 100% cotton batting, medium weight

Sewing machine and related supplies, including matching thread

1 skein embroidery floss in the color of your choice

Large embroidery needle

Erasable fabric marker

Acrylic ruler or yardstick

Canvas drop cloth

Towel (if working on the floor)

Artist tape (if working on the floor)

NOTE: Shot cotton is a loosely woven fabric with the warp yarn in one color and the weft in another. This creates a special vibrancy—a "shot" of color. Shot cotton is a perfect canvas for painting because the loose weave takes the pigment well and the depth of the color provides a nice base for any pattern. It is best to use a separate paintbrush for each color of paint.

PREPARE TO PAINT

1. Cut the shot cotton to 44" x 60" (1.1 x 1.5 m), iron to remove all wrinkles, and set aside. Use the remaining fabric for test painting.

2. Cover your workspace with a canvas drop cloth; ideally you would do this project on a large tabletop that is about 4' (1.2 m) long. If you need to work on the floor, have a towel handy to fold up to put under your knees for comfort. (I painted on a table while sitting down and folded the unpainted length of the fabric in my lap to keep it off the floor. If you work on the floor, lay the quilt top flat and gently tape the edges to your drop cloth so the cotton will not shift during painting.)

3. Mix your colors: I added approximately 1 tablespoon (14.8 ml) of water per 3 tablespoons (44.3 ml) of paint for each color I used. Test your colors on the leftover fabric, using a separate brush for each color. Make sure to let the paint dry completely on the fabric, as the colors will dry up to a half-shade lighter on the cotton. Adjust your paint-to-water ratio as needed to achieve your desired colors.

A. Paint squares with ruler as guide

B. Complete color grid

C. Add knots of floss, if desired

ADD THE PATTERN

4. Work from left to right along the shorter edge of the quilt top, beginning about 1" (2.5 cm) from the top and 2" (5.1 cm) from the side. Paint a row of 4" (10.2 cm) squares of color across the quilt top, leaving a 1" (2.5 cm) border between each square, alternating the colors as you go. Use your ruler as a guide, but be sure to clean it as needed so you do not drag paint across the quilt top. **(A)**

5. Allow the paint to dry—use a hair dryer to speed up the process if you like—and then fold the painted portion of the quilt top like an accordion so another swath of blank fabric is revealed. Continue in this fashion until you have covered the entire quilt top with a 3-color grid pattern. **(B)**

6. When the quilt top is dry, heat-set according to the manufacturer's instructions and set aside.

COMPLETE THE PROJECT

7. To make the quilt, cut the backing fabric to the dimensions of the quilt top. Place the two pieces right sides together and lay the cotton batting on top. Smooth out any wrinkles and trim as needed to square the edges. Pin all sides together.

8. Using a ½" (1.3 cm) seam allowance, stitch the layers together, leaving an opening approximately 16" (40.6 cm) long at the bottom for turning. Add an extra pin at the end of the opening to help you remember to stop stitching.

9. Clip the corners of the quilt, trim as needed, and turn it right-side out through the opening. Iron the edges of the quilt so they are flat and crisp; press the edges of the opening under and pin together.

10. Starting at a corner, topstitch around the entire perimeter of the quilt with a ¼" (6 mm) seam allowance.

11. Use an erasable fabric marker to mark the spots where you will add knots of embroidery floss, if desired. Add knots about every 10" (25.4 cm). To make a knot, thread the embroidery needle and stitch through from the top, leaving about a 3" (7.6 cm) tail, and then stitch back through from the underside, approximately ¼" (6 mm) away. Tie a double knot and then trim the floss, leaving a small ¼" (6 mm) tail. **(C)**

12. Add knots at every marked spot. Remove any erasable marker according to the manufacturer's instructions. The hand-painted quilt top is colorfast, but I recommend washing by hand as befits an heirloom.

SOLAR PRINT SCARF

SUN PRINTS ARE MAGICAL. IT IS THRILLING TO WATCH THE PALE FABRIC TURN A BRILLIANT COLOR IN THE SUN AND SEE THE BEAUTIFUL PATTERNS FORMED BY THE OBJECTS THAT BLOCKED THE LIGHT. THIS PROJECT USES THE SAME MAGICAL LIGHT-SENSITIVE PROCESS TO MAKE A DRAMATIC SCARF FROM SOFT COTTON VOILE. HERE I USED PENNIES AS RESISTS TO MAKE A RANDOM POLKA-DOT DESIGN.

SURFACE & SUPPLIES

2 yards (1.8 m) pale-colored cotton voile, at least 54" (1.3 m) wide

4 bottles light-sensitive dye in the color of your choice (I used Jacquard SolarFast in Blue)

1 bottle scour detergent (I used Jacquard SolarFast Wash)

300 pennies (or similar-sized round objects)

Tape measure or yardstick

Scissors

3" (7.6 cm) paintbrush (or larger)

Glass jar or bowl

Plastic drop cloth

Needle and matching thread (or sewing machine and related supplies)

NOTE: This is a project for a sunny day. You can either work outside or in a room where you can place your scarf in front of a light source, such as a large bright window. If you are working indoors, you need adequate ventilation. The intensity of your fabric color and the clarity of your prints will vary depending on how much light you have. If you are working inside and the light is somewhat muted, the final result will be rather muted as well. Your test swatches of cotton will help you decide how long your design should be exposed to bright light, based on how saturated you want the color and how crisp you want the pattern.

PREPARE TO PAINT

1. Cut your voile into a large square based on the width of the fabric. For instance, if your cotton is 54" (1.3 m) wide, cut a 54" (1.3 m) square, incorporating the selvage of the fabric as one side of the scarf. The scarf in this project is 56" x 56" (1.4 x 1.4 m).

2. Cut the remaining yardage into test swatches no smaller than 6" (15.2 cm) square. When you are cutting, be mindful that the fabric could be used again as napkins, or for other sewing and craft projects, so cut them carefully.

3. Lay your plastic drop cloth out on the ground if outside, or on a table or the floor in front of a sunny window.

4. Working in the shade, pour the dye into a glass jar or bowl and submerge your paintbrush. Paint the dye onto your cotton swatches, making sure that it penetrates the fabric and soaks in. Take your pennies and scatter them over the ink-soaked cotton swatches. **(A)**

5. Move the swatches into the sun and leave them out until the fabric is the desired shade of blue. I suggest leaving groups of swatches in the light for varying amounts of time so you can judge the results before you work on your final project. Leave the first batch out for just a few minutes and work from there; you may want to make notes for reference.

6. When the swatches have reached your desired shade, pick up the cotton with the pennies still in place and dunk it into a sink filled with very hot water. (You can retrieve your pennies when the swatches are clean!) Add 1 or 2 capfuls of the scour detergent (or the amount the manufacturer suggests) and rinse your test swatches with the hottest water possible, agitating constantly, with the water flowing for at least 10 minutes. When the color is fixed, rinse it clean in cool water.

7. While your test swatches are drying, use damp paper towels to clean all excess dye off the drop cloth, making sure it is clean and dry before you begin working on your scarf.

8. Look over your swatches and choose your favorite to mimic for your final scarf.

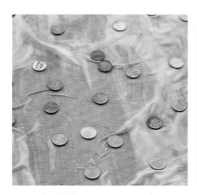

A. Make a test swatch

B. Apply pigment to scarf fabric

C. Arrange resists in a pleasing manner

ADD THE PATTERN AND FINISH

9. In the shade, spread out your scarf fabric on the drop cloth and brush on the dye. I chose to apply the dye in a loose and painterly fashion so the texture of the brushstrokes is visible in the final project. **(B)**

10. Create the polka-dot pattern by making loose rows with the pennies, leaving 1" or 2" (2.5 to 5.1 cm) between each penny. There are several advantages to using pennies in this project: They make perfectly round dots and the weight of the coins helps keep everything flat while you are working on your pattern. I began in the top right corner of my scarf and followed the edge of the fabric as a guide.

11. Continue until the entire surface of the scarf is covered in pennies and then look over your design for any empty or crowded areas that may need a penny added (or removed); adjust your design as needed. **(C)**

12. Expose in the sun long enough to reach your desired shade of blue, lifting up a penny after a few minutes to see the clarity of your print. Roll up the wet scarf, dump the pennies into a container, and then scour with detergent in your sink or washing machine as in step 6, following the manufacturer's directions. Rinse the scarf with clean water and allow to dry.

13. Make a narrow hem along the edges of the scarf by hand or machine. Machine wash your scarf before wearing.

Play with different resists to create interesting patterns.

WINDSWEPT BEDDING SET

CLASSIC STRIPES ARE GIVEN A TWIST HERE, WITH FREEFORM LINES THAT SEEM TO HAVE BEEN BLOWN BY THE WIND. THE SATURATED COLORS MAKE FOR A SMART PAIRING, AND THE PATTERN IS SIMPLE TO PAINT, YET THE RESULTS ARE REMARKABLE. THIS PROJECT TAKES SOME TIME AND A LITTLE BIT OF EXTRA PLANNING TO COMPLETE ONLY BECAUSE OF THE LARGE SCALE, BUT ONCE YOU BEGIN THE PAINTING MOVES QUICKLY.

SURFACE & SUPPLIES

100% cotton white duvet cover and 2 pillowcases (I used a full/queen duvet cover)

Textile paints in 2 colors of your choice (I used two jars each of Jacquard Dye-Na-Flow in Golden Yellow and Pewter)

2 round paintbrushes with pointed tips, each ¾" (1.9 cm) wide

1 yard (91.5 cm) 100% cotton or an old all-cotton bed sheet for test painting

2 clear plastic drop cloths, each 9' x 12' (2.7 x 3.7 m)

Newsprint or kraft paper

Artist tape

Spray bottle filled with water

Paper towels or clean rag

Yardstick

20" x 30" (50.8 x 76.2 cm) piece of foam core board

Permanent marker

Towel or kneepads (optional)

4 large safety pins

PREPARE TO PAINT (PILLOWCASES)

1. To paint the test swatches and pillowcases, cover your tabletop with newsprint or kraft paper to protect the surface. You may want to work on the floor to paint the duvet cover.

2. Cut your test fabric into 20" x 30" (50.8 x 76.2 cm) rectangles so they are the same size as your pillowcases; this will give you an accurate idea of scale when working on the stripes. Tape the corners of the test fabric to your work surface so the fabric is taut. Gently mist with water until the fabric is slightly damp and cool to the touch. If your fabric is too wet, blot it with a paper towel or clean rag until the cotton is uniformly damp.

3. Place your yardstick at one upper corner of the test fabric and angle it at approximately 45°. Dip your brush into the jar of yellow paint, shake to remove the excess, and paint diagonal lines, using the yardstick as a guide. (Each time you place the loaded brush on the wet fabric, it will leave the pleasing "pool" of ink you see in the pattern.) Leave about ½" (1.3 cm) between your brush and the yardstick. Be sure to place a rag or paper towel under the brush when you move it across your fabric to catch drips.

4. Move the yardstick about 4" (10.2 cm) and paint another yellow diagonal stripe.

5. Repeat steps 3 and 4 with gray paint and the second paintbrush, placing the gray stripes in between the yellow ones so the colors alternate. Continue to paint the entire piece. **(A)**

6. Wash all your project linens in cold water to remove any starch and dry for about 20 minutes. Remove them when they are slightly damp, but not wet. Start this process while you are testing your materials to speed the project along.

A. Make a test print

B. Insert board into pillowcase

C. Paint yellow stripes

ADD THE PATTERN (PILLOWCASES)

7. Slip the foam core board inside a pillowcase so that the fabric is taut. **(B)** Follow the instructions outlined in steps 3–5 and paint alternating yellow and gray stripes. **(C + D)**

8. When finished painting, gently remove the board. If there is any ink on the board, wipe away with a paper towel or rag. Repeat step 7 to paint the second pillowcase. Hang or lay flat to dry.

D. Paint gray stripes

E. Trace duvet cover onto drop cloth

F. Add allover stripes

PREPARE TO PAINT (DUVET COVER)

9. Before you begin, be sure that the duvet cover has been prepared as in step 6.

10. Place one of the drop cloths on your work surface and smooth out the wrinkles as best you can. Tape each corner down so the plastic will not move, then lay the second drop cloth on top. Tape down the corners. Place the duvet cover atop both layers. Use a permanent marker and the yardstick to trace around the perimeter of the duvet cover, marking directly on the top drop cloth. **(E)**

11. Cut the top drop cloth along the lines you drew in step 10, so your sheet of plastic is the same size as your duvet cover. Carefully place it inside the duvet cover to protect the bottom layer while you are painting. Pin the plastic in place at all four corners so it will not slip as you work.

ADD THE PATTERN (DUVET COVER)

12. If the duvet cover is no longer damp, mist it with water and blot with paper towels or a clean rag until it is cool to the touch as the pillowcases were. (If you are working on the floor, you may want to use a folded towel or kneepads for comfort.)

13. Follow the instructions in steps 3–5 and begin painting the stripes. Since the duvet cover is so much larger than the pillowcases, you will need to slide the yardstick from one side to the other as you work, wiping away paint from the yardstick with a rag as you go. Mist the cotton with water as needed, but avoid spraying the wet stripes themselves. **(F)**

14. Continue painting until the entire duvet cover is decorated with alternating stripes.

COMPLETE THE PROJECT

15. When the duvet cover and paint are both completely dry, remove the safety pins from the corners and the plastic sheet from inside. Follow the manufacturer's instructions to heat-set the textile paint. Wash your new bedding alone once before you launder it with other items.

TEMPLATES

Floral Tote Bag, page 66

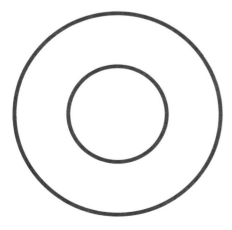

Folk Art Barn Lamp, page 74

Modern Side Chair, page 77

Circles Linen Apron, page 26

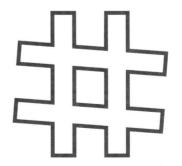

Crosshatch Zippered Pouch,
page 34

Modern Side Chair, page 77

Silk Infinity Scarf, page 82

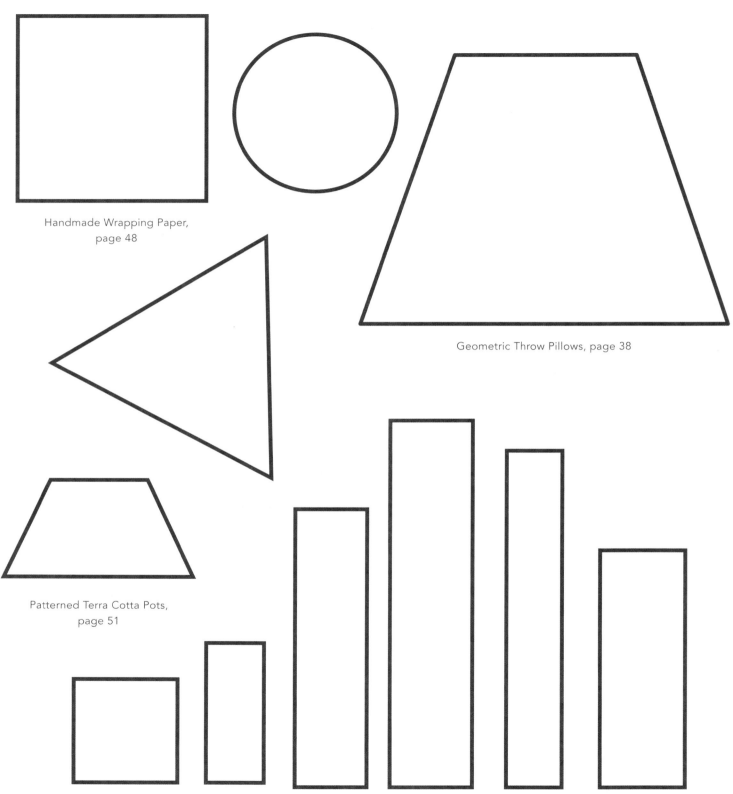

Handmade Wrapping Paper,
page 48

Geometric Throw Pillows, page 38

Patterned Terra Cotta Pots,
page 51

Starburst Wall Prints
page 94

Cozy Beach Towels, page 30

Blooming Market Bags, page 42

Bright Table Linens,
page 70

Bonus template

RESOURCES

THE TOOLS AND MATERIALS USED FOR THE PROJECTS IN THIS BOOK ARE AVAILABLE AT WELL-STOCKED ART AND CRAFT SUPPLY STORES NATIONWIDE. IF YOU CANNOT FIND WHAT YOU ARE LOOKING FOR IN YOUR AREA, HERE IS A LIST OF ONLINE RESOURCES.

COLLAGE

Collage stocks all of the art supplies used in this book.
www.collagepdx.com

DHARMA TRADING CO.

This company carries moldable foam stamps and many other stamping and printing supplies, as well as natural fiber project blanks perfect for items printed or painted by hand.
www.dharmatrading.com

DICK BLICK ART MATERIALS

Dick Blick carries a comprehensive selection of printmaking and painting supplies.
www.dickblick.com

IKEA

IKEA has a vast array of stylish and inexpensive housewares, textiles, and furniture, all of which are well suited to the projects in this book.
www.ikea.com

FOG LINEN WORK

The linen apron used for the Circles Linen Apron on page 26 is available from Fog Linen Work. They make linen products for bed, bath, kitchen, and wardrobe, and these items make a perfect surface for any of the textile projects in this book.
www.shop-foglinen.com

JACQUARD PRODUCTS

Jacquard makes an expansive line of pigments for use on all manner of textiles. Their products are available in well-stocked art and craft stores and online.
www.jacquardproducts.com

MCCLAIN'S PRINTMAKING SUPPLIES

McClain's Printmaking Supplies carries everything you need for traditional relief printmaking, including a large selection of high-quality carving tools.
www.imcclains.com

MICHAELS STORES

Michaels is a good place to go for paints, brushes, and other crafting and printing supplies.
www.michaels.com

PURL SOHO

Purl Soho carries a beautiful array of fabrics, including cotton prints and solids. They ship worldwide.
www.purlsoho.com

TANDY LEATHER FACTORY

This site has wide range of leathers and leather working tools.
www.tandyleatherfactory.com

WEST ELM

West Elm is a great place to find a large selection of quality ceramics, baskets, and textiles at reasonable prices.
www.westelm.com

ACKNOWLEDGMENTS

It has been my profound honor to work on this project, and the making of this book would not have been possible without the support of my family, friends, and colleagues.

Thank you to my editor, Melanie Falick, for seeing a book inside of me that I did not know was there yet, and for giving me the creative freedom to make it come to life. Without her encouragement and guiding hand this book would not have happened. She was never too busy to give sage words of advice, calm the nerves of a first-time author, and steer me on the right track.

Technical editor Valerie Shrader helped organize and clarify each and every instruction. Her warmth, humor, and attention to detail made the process a pleasure, and I know this is a better book because she worked on it.

Book designer Brooke Reynolds is someone I had admired from afar long before this book was written, and I admire her even more after having had the pleasure of working with her. I could not have imagined anyone else designing this book.

Thank you to my photography team-—Lisa Warninger for the beautiful photographs and magical energy, Chelsea Fuss for her styling genius, and Amber Furqueron for her tireless work and lovely smile. I feel so fortunate to have had such a talented group of women by my side during this process. Their care and attention to each and every photograph fills me with deep gratitude and joy. Even though we worked from sun up until sundown, our time at the beach was one of my very favorite "vacations" ever. Kara Jean, you were the perfect model and a delight.

Fran, John, and Remy's beautiful beach house and the Ace Hotel Portland provided endless inspiration, and I cannot envision these photographs taken at any other locations.

Thank you to Maria Raleigh and the entire staff at Collage in Portland. It is the best arts and crafts store I have ever had the pleasure of visiting, and their generosity and enthusiasm for this project was overwhelming. I simply adore all of you!

West Elm donated many of the beautiful items I stamped, stenciled, and painted for this book. Thank you!

I would like to thank Rena Tom for being my mentor, and for believing in my work from the very beginning. Rena's sound, honest advice laid the foundation for this book.

Adam and Jamie, thank you for helping to keep my business running during this crazy year.

My incredible community of friends inspired and supported me, and I love all of you. Special thanks to Colleen for donating her time and talents, Jessica for so many playdates and stylish props, Dane for laughter, and Sarah because I have always needed a sister.

And, finally, I could not have made this book without the unwavering support of my family. My daughters, Angelina and Iris, encouraged me every step of the way. They never complained when my studio took over most of the house and I spent so many long hours working and distracted. I love you both with all of my heart.

There are no words for the amount of love and patience my husband, Victor, showed me throughout this process. This project would not have been possible without him, and I love him even more now than I did when I started this book.

And I must thank my father, who taught me about having character, getting back up again when I fell down, and the importance of a sense of humor. Even in his absence he showed me that inspiration could be greater than grief.

Last but not least, I must express my gratitude to my mother, Kacey, who gave me the gift of time to work on this project. My mother is an incredible artist, printmaker, and teacher. Her unconditional love and support has been a constant in my life and she taught me almost everything I know about being an artist and a mother, and why I should cherish each role with equal measure. Thank you.

ANNA JOYCE is is an artist, textile designer, and teacher based in Portland, OR. She designs an eponymous line of hand-printed products for wardrobe and home. Her work has been featured in *Lucky*, *Real Simple*, *Anthology*, and *Mollie Makes* magazines, and on an array of design blogs, including Martha Stewart, Design*Sponge, Oh Joy!, and SF Girl By Bay. She has a bachelor of fine arts degree in printmaking from the California College of the Arts. Visit her website at annajoycedesign.com.